ROAD TRIP WITH REMINGTON BEAGLE

MICHIGAN TO ALASKA AND BACK

By Valerie Winans

PUBLICATION CONSULTANTS
We Believe In The Power Of Authors

PO Box 221974 Anchorage, Alaska 99522-1974
books@publicationconsultants.com—www.publicationconsultants.com

ISBN Number: 978-1-59433-802-1
eBook ISBN Number: 978-1-59433-803-8

Manufactured in the United States of America

Dedicated to my daughters:
Lisa, Wendy, Natalie, Kimberly, and Marcia.

Also by

Valerie Winans
Alaska's Savage River

CONTENTS

	Preface	9
Chapter 1.	Life is an Adventure	15
Chapter 2.	On the Road	21
Chapter 3.	O Canada	25
Chapter 4.	Back in the Good Ole' USA	39
Chapter 5.	Our New Address	45
Chapter 6.	Living and Working at Savage River	55
Chapter 7.	Fishing in Ferry and Homer	61
Chapter 8.	Savage Cabin and Savage Loop Trail	71
Chapter 9.	Fairbanks	75
Chapter 10.	Nenana	91
Chapter 11.	The Trestle	93
Chapter 12.	Flying Fixed-Wing	97
Chapter 13.	Riding the Shuttle Bus	101
Chapter 14.	A Trip to Barrow	105
Chapter 15.	Fun Things in and Near the Park	111
Chapter 16.	Flowers, Birds, and Bears	115
Chapter 17.	Four Wheeling and Exploring	125
Chapter 18.	Denali Highway and Valdez	131
Chapter 19.	Skagway	139
Chapter 20.	Hope and Whittier	143
Chapter 21.	Kenai	149
Chapter 22.	Seward	153
Chapter 23.	Willow and Wasilla	161
Chapter 24.	Palmer and Hatcher Pass	163
Chapter 25.	Anchorage	165
Chapter 26.	Going Home	169
Chapter 27.	Home Sweet Home	173

PREFACE

The three of us, Dave, Val, and I, fell in love with Alaska, and especially Savage Campground, during our halcyon days of working in the park. Almost from the beginning of our stay, Val was on a search for information about the special, magical place where we worked and lived for two seasons.

In her quest for all things Savage River, she could only find bits and pieces of information. And, as she shared what she learned with others, Val realized that she was not the only one with interest. I'm not sure exactly when she decided to write a book, but I do remember a man called Tom Walker visiting our campsite. Val had read several of his books and had written to him for advice. Mr. Walker was gracious enough to encourage Val to write about Savage Campground. He said that the book needed to be written, and he suggested she could use the University of Alaska Fairbanks' archives for research.

After that, Val was on a mission to do research for a book. She started by meeting with Jane Bryant, the cultural anthropologist for the park at that time. Next, we traveled to Fairbanks to see what could be gleaned from the archives.

We stayed at Pike's Landing. Pike's accommodated gentlemen beagles, which I am. We enjoyed sitting on the deck and watching the boats go by on the Chena River. Having a television in the room was a novelty for Dave and Val because they had been without the infernal machine all summer. Personally, I didn't miss it. Most of the stuff on TV is of no interest to anyone with a brain.

While doing research at the archives, Val was connected with a local philanthropist, Candy Waugaman, who not only provided information and pictures, but connected us to a wonderful woman, Frances Erickson, who had firsthand information on life in the original Savage Camp. Candy also gave Val an index of newspaper articles that could be accessed through the archives, which proved to be a huge help. Val was very excited to schedule an interview with Frances.

Val arrived at the home of Frances Erickson with a tape recorder because she did not want to miss anything that Frances shared. When Val first talked with Frances, Frances said she didn't think she would have anything worthwhile to tell, but the time flew by and left Val with a treasure chest of information. Frances had lived at Savage Camp every summer from the age of three to thirteen. She had so much to offer in terms of the place and the people. She knew the Karstens family, she knew Grant Pearson, Lena and Johnny Howard, and her favorite— other than her father—was Lou Corbley. Even though Frances was just a child at the time, she followed others around and helped out wherever she could. She remembered when Count Ilia Tolstoy visited the park; she said he was a very fine man. Frances told Val about riding horses to the park from Lignite, where they were housed every winter. When Frances explained the route they took to the park, Val was astonished because we had seen some of that route on the banks of the Savage River. It was unimaginable that someone rode horses through there. I would not even want to walk it. Frances had a special horse she rode near Savage Camp, and sometimes there were places the horse would not take her. She surmised that the horse smelled a bear or another dangerous animal nearby.

I'm sure he did. I have gotten scents of bear in the park that made the hair on my back stand up. It is a wild and dangerous smell. Once I got the scent of a lynx and connected the smell with a sighting of the wild cat. It was still exciting, but no longer felt dangerous to me. On the other paw, bear scent always remained dangerous for me, and wolf too. Even though wolves are my distant relation, they are scary. Beagles, through domestication, have become what some call *tamed*, although I prefer to think of it as *sophistication*. The English contributed to our intellect, and I still salivate at the mention of tea and crumpets.

Back at the park, Jane Lakeman, the park historian and archivist, shared pictures and information. While there, one of her assistants suggested that Val contact Jack Coghill. Jack's father was a friend of Bobby Sheldon, and Jack's family vacationed at Savage River almost every year while Jack was growing up.

Val phoned Jack Coghill and was surprised to get an invitation to visit him at his home in Nenana, Alaska. Mr. Coghill was a distinguished member of Alaska's society and a contributor to its history. He not only served as mayor of Nenana for twenty-three years, he was a State legislator and helped write the Alaska Constitution before the territory became a state. He was also Lieutenant Governor of Alaska. Jack Coghill welcomed us into his home like we were long-lost relatives. We had a remarkable afternoon listening to his stories.

Jack told us that he and his family would travel from Nenana to Savage Camp via the Brill Car. The Brill Car was a special passenger car of the Alaska Railroad. The *Fairbanks Daily News–Miner* advertised a trip from Nenana to Savage Camp:

"The Big Brill Car of the Alaska Railroad, capable of transporting fifty passengers with comfort, will leave here about 12:30 o'clock Saturday afternoon, and returning will arrive here about 11 o'clock Sunday night. The fare, including all expenses of the trip, such as transportation to the Savage River Camp of the park, and return, subsistence and lodging during the stay, is announced to be $22.10, which is considered a very material reduction over the usual cost of such an outing. Automobiles will meet the car and will transport the excursionists to this camp. The park company, under the direction of Messrs. James L. Galen and Robert E. Sheldon, will offer novel entertainment, including a real rodeo carrying all the thrills of the wild west. For this feature a bronco buster, hailing from Hollywood, California, has been provided. Two mean, rarin' cayuses are in process of grooming for the spectacle."

You can easily understand why a young boy would be excited about such a trip. Jack reminisced about the social hall where the camp had a Victrola that played "78 platters." He remembered Bobby Sheldon taking them by horse and wagon to the head of the Savage River. He recalled that Count Ilia Tolstoy was "a well-groomed gentleman." He knew Grant Pearson, as well as Johnny and Lena Howard. He also recalled the moving of the horses from Lignite to Savage Camp and back again in the fall. He remembered that in the late fall they would take the horses through the drying riverbed through the Savage River Valley back to Lignite.

Jack's parents owned the general store in Nenana. Growing up, Jack helped in the store. He asked us if we knew what it was to quarter eggs. Val had no idea, and neither did I. Jack explained that much of what they sold in their store reached them by barge. Nenana is located at the confluence of the Nenana and Tanana Rivers, and every year the rivers freeze. The last barge in the fall would bring them everything they would get until the ice broke up in the spring, including dozens of eggs. The Coghills would store the eggs in their basement where it was cold, but the eggs did not freeze. Every few days, Jack and his siblings would go to the basement to quarter the eggs. They picked up each egg and turned it one-quarter turn and put it back. This turning of the eggs kept the yolks in the center of the eggs and allowed them to last four months or more. They also periodically candled the eggs, and if the eggs started to get cloudy they would take them upstairs where their mother would bake something using the eggs and sell the baked goods in the store. That was a tidbit of trivia you won't often find. By the way, I like eggs if they are scrambled … with cheese … and pieces of bacon.

As we were getting ready to leave Jack's house, he gave Val a signed copy of Alaska's Constitution. Val was pleased with this gift from Mr. Coghill, but one sniff was enough for me.

The people with personal memories of Savage Camp in its early days are getting fewer each day. Their memories enhanced the history for us, and also gave us a bit of the spirit of that special place called Savage Camp.

In 2014, Val's book, *Alaska's Savage River: Inside Denali National Park and Preserve,* was published. (It is available on Amazon in both paperback and e-book editions.) The experiences we shared while traveling to and from Alaska, while we lived in the park, and during our explorations of Alaska on our days off inspired me to do a travel blog. Fans of the travel blog grew as time went on. Some have expressed disappointment that *Alaska's Savage River* was not the blog revisited. So Val has inspired me to share my experiences in my own special way about our travels.

Remington Beagle

CHAPTER ONE

LIFE IS AN ADVENTURE

"Instead of trying to make your life perfect, give yourself the freedom to make it an adventure, and go ever upward."
Drew Houston

My name is Remington Beagle. I am a fourteen-inch beagle; which makes me taller than Uno, the famous Westminster Dog Show winner, but still a recognized AKC hound. I am unusual in the beagle world because I rarely bark. I do not feel the need to bark because both of my humans meet my every need—sometimes before I even know I have one. These humans are thoroughly in love with me, from the freckles on my cute little nose to the tip of my often-wagging tail. I graduated from puppy school and consider myself an intellectual and raconteur.

The first time I heard my humans talking about going to Alaska it was very confusing. I knew that something was going on because they began to scurry back and forth between the house and travel trailer every day.

I like the trailer. Even though it is a small living space, it has good smells. Dogs have a much greater appreciation of smells than humans. For example, my favorite smells range from steak on the grill to another dog's butt. So, when I go into the trailer and give it a sniff, all I can tell you is that the smells are good.

My problem with the trailer is that it is attached to the pickup truck. My problem with the pickup is that when it moves, it makes me sick. When I am forced into the truck, I start to drool—even before the truck moves—in anticipation of the actual moving and subsequent regurgitation. Dave and Val, my humans, are fully aware of my problem. I knew we were off on an adventure when early one morning they forced a Dramamine down my throat, lifted me into the backseat of the truck, and we drove off.

Traveling by car, it is a two-hour trip from Traverse City, Michigan, to the bridge at the Straits of Mackinac, no matter which way you go. It's all two-lane roads, so you may as well drive highway US-31 because it has the best views. US-31 North twists and turns around orchards and woodlands, and there are occasional glimpses of Lake Michigan; sometimes within a few feet of the road. Following the shoreline, around the curve of the bay, there are houses and buildings in the foreground, but as your eye follows the horizon, the houses blend into the forest. The undulating dark green of pine tree forests separates the land from the blue of the water and sky. From hilltops, a traveler can discern gradations of color, from pastels near the shoreline to deeper blues and greens as the water deepens. Sunlight sparkles on the big lake and the view is pleasing, but I am still most interested in olfactory opportunities.

Sniffing opportunities are few while in the cab of a pickup truck. Val's coffee is often predominant, but that just makes me more nauseous. When the truck slows down Dave will sometimes open the back window, so I can stick my head out for a breath of fresh air. That is not only helpful for my motion issue; it also presents a litany of smells for identification. I am now able to classify road kill according to odor: skunk of course, raccoon, opossum, and an occasional white tailed deer.

Mackinac Bridge

When you have gone as far north as you can in the Lower Peninsula of Michigan, you will reach the Straits of Mackinac. The Mackinac Bridge has spanned the gap between the Lower and Upper peninsulas since the 1950s. Before then, the only way across was by boat. Val says that she remembers going across the straits by ferry when she was a kid. Cars lined up to get on the ferry, and it was a lengthy process, as you can imagine. Back then, some people were against the idea of building a bridge because they wanted to keep the Upper Peninsula the way it was, which was rural and rustic.

Since the bridge opened, the Upper Peninsula has changed a lot, and some of those changes have been good while others not so good. Regardless, the distance between the shores remains the same. Michiganders refer to this five-mile engineering wonder as "the bridge," as if it was the only bridge there is. These are the same people who point at the top of their index finger to indicate the Straits of Mackinaw. I don't get it.

On the days when there are strong winds, travelers are escorted across to ensure that their speed is kept at twenty miles per hour. Val doesn't really like driving, or for that matter riding, on the bridge. She especially doesn't like being on the lane that is a grate. She says there is something wrong about being that high in the air and being able to look straight down to the water hundreds of feet below. Instead of looking down and getting dizzy, she should check out the horizon. There are beautiful islands to see, and boats leaving their white frothing wake as contrast to the deep blue of the water. I'm a good one to give advice – Dramamine is the only reason I am not curled in a ball with my eyes shut.

I love the bridge. With the window down, even a little bit, the smells are amazing. Humans can only get a sense of moisture in the air and minimal scents of water and fish. Dogs, and especially beagles, get hundreds of savory scents. As Dave drove the truck across the bridge, Val closed her eyes and I jumped from side to side, window to window, trying not to miss anything. I thought we reached St. Ignace way too soon. Val disagreed.

Once we crossed into the Upper Peninsula, we made a swing to the west on US-2, which snakes along the northern shore of Lake Michigan for many miles. For a while, sand dunes are evident on both sides of the road, and sometimes sand even accumulates in the road. There are many spots along this stretch where travelers pull over and go for a swim in Lake Michigan. I'm glad we didn't stop because I am definitely not a water dog. As far as I'm concerned, water is for drinking—period.

We passed wetlands, dunes, and forests. After Brevort and before we reached Epoufette, the Cut River Bridge greeted us. It is not as magnificent as the Mackinac Bridge, but spectacular in its own right. It spans a gap over the Cut River, one hundred and forty-seven feet below. There are roadside parks on both sides of the bridge and a staircase that leads down to the river. But remember, what walks down must walk back up.

Naubinway was next, and it is one of our favorite places because that is where my human sister and her husband have a cabin. Naubinway is the northernmost community on Lake Michigan and is the largest Upper Peninsula commercial fishing port on the Great Lakes. Fresh and smoked fish is available when in season. Other Naubinway attractions include the Top of the Lake Snowmobile Museum, the 906 Store, Hiawatha National Forest, and the beautiful Milikioka River where it empties into Lake Michigan. My favorite is the sugar-sand beach where a beagle can pick up the smell of rotting vegetation, an occasional dead fish or crustacean, and maybe even the neighbor's cat. I think it's Siamese because its scat has an aroma of sushi.

East of Rapid River, Dave said, "Look! Sandhill cranes! They are standing so still, I thought they were yard ornaments." I looked out the window, and I would have thought they were yard ornaments too if they had not moved. It was amazing how awkward they are on the ground compared to how beautiful they are in flight. I wanted to get out and chase them, just a little, but we drove by them so fast I only had time to get a glimpse.

The only way I knew we had left Michigan was when I saw the sign welcoming us to Wisconsin. We crossed the northern part of the state and, before long, we were in Superior, Wisconsin, which is just across the river from Duluth, Minnesota. This is where the St. Louis River empties into Lake Superior. While crossing from Wisconsin into

Minnesota on one bridge, several other bridges are in sight. When I think of Duluth, I think of bridges. There was a turn we did not want to miss just on the other side of the bridge, so we were vigilant. There was a sense of accomplishment after Dave negotiated the turns and we realized we were on track to our destination for the evening.

The Saginaw Campground in Saginaw, Minnesota, is all about location, location, location. There are pull-through sites where Dave can park without unhooking the trailer from the truck—super convenient for a one-night stay. The price was reasonable; the showers were clean, with lots of hot water for Val; and there was even a small patch of grass between the sites for dog relaxation.

Just as we settled down for the night, we heard a train. What is it with campgrounds and railroads? Thankfully that was the last train we heard before we fell asleep. I was especially thankful because Val gets grouchy when she has not had enough sleep. It's a human thing. Beagles are good-natured and never grouchy—sleep or no sleep.

CHAPTER 2

ON THE ROAD

"When you rise in the morning, give thanks for the light, for your life, for your strength. Give thanks for your food and for the joy of living. If you see no reason to give thanks, the fault lies in yourself."
                                                                    Tecumseh

Our plan was to reach Minot, North Dakota, by the end of the day. On the way there, we drove through Rugby, North Dakota. *Do you know what Rugby is famous for? It is the geographical center of the North American continent. Pretty cool, huh?*

As we drove through eastern North Dakota, we saw large rolling plains and huge farms. A lot of corn is grown in this area. As we neared Minot, the hills got bigger and the road higher.

There are choices for where to camp near Minot. One is Swenson's Valley View RV Park, right on the highway, which was a plus. It sits on a bluff above the town, which makes the view spectacular. But my favorite, and where we decided to stay, is the Roughrider Campground, located only a short distance off of US-2 west of Minot. Roughrider is on the Souris River and has big, shady lots; wonderful showers; and friendly people who operate it.

After we set up camp and had our supper, we decided to sit outside for a while. We couldn't help but notice that there was a dog barking nearby. He was so hysterical I couldn't even tell what he was saying. Some dogs have no manners whatsoever. I only bark when it is absolutely necessary. Like when Dave pets the neighbor's cat.

Communication between man and his best friend can be complex. In order for communication to occur, there must be understanding on some level between both parties. A pat on the head and the resultant wag of the tail demonstrates touch communication: "Good dog," from the human and "Happy, happy," from the dog. Levels of exchange go up from there.

Much of my understanding of the spoken word is derived from the tone of the human voice. I know that loud expletives mean something bad happened. On the other hand, anything said softly, especially in baby talk, means something was good; very good. As a puppy, I learned that when a human raises his or her tone at the end of a word, the result is a question that I am required to answer with body language.

"Cook*ie*?"

Oh, yes! A wag of my tail; maybe a little jump or two.

"Supp*er*?"

Sure. But my response depended on what was being offered. Chicken gets the full Monty.

"*Walk*?"

Running and fetching the leash works.

A beagle's howl is a beautiful sound, which I reserve for very special occasions when I need to get my humans' attention. Usually a whine with a tip of my head produces a positive result.

My humans have been skillful in sharing their language. One of our earliest understandings was where the doggy bathroom is located. Being as smart as I am, I learned right away that the potty spot is outdoors, which begged the question How do I get there? The whine and tip of the head could result in a litany of questions from Dave and Val as they tried to define what I wanted. Val came up with a solution. She tied a bell to the backdoor—hung low enough for me to hit it with my paw. She showed me how to hit it, and then gave me a treat and put me outside each time I would hit the bell. Well, Pavlov had nothing on Val. It worked great! When I want outside, I ring the bell. When we travel, Val hangs the bell inside the trailer and our communication system continues. Perfect.

In the morning, we continued westward. The vistas were expansive, and only interrupted by the road we were on. Dave mused about what it would have been like to travel by horse, with no road to guide you, 150 or 200 years ago. Just as we started to feel like pioneers, we began to see oil wells near the road. Lots of oil wells. Then cattle ranches with oil wells. Next, we spotted a few antelope; then entire herds of antelope. Once again, there was a failure to communicate because I was desperately signaling that I wanted to get out and chase them. Dave and Val were clueless—or at least pretended to be.

Fort Belknap Casino, at the junction of Highway 2 and 66 in Montana, was cause for a stop. Dave and Val ate their lunch there and couldn't resist gambling for a short time. Dave won $21 and Val won $9. *Who says there is no such thing as a free lunch?* I got a walk with a potty break and a nice drink of water. No antelope though.

Our goal for the day was to reach Shelby, Montana. After a stop for fuel and to repair a blown tire in Havre, we located the Lewis and Clark Campground, high on a hill just outside of Shelby. From the campground we could see a large windmill farm. We thought it must really be churning out electricity because the wind was howling. We couldn't even stand to be outside for long due to the whipping wind, which was okay because we were tired after a long day on the road. All we wanted to do was eat and then sleep.

While we are on the road, eating is just for fueling the engine of the body. Val hates to cook on a good day; so, after traveling all day and setting up camp, she is in no mood to attempt a rendition of Martha Stewart. Opening a cardboard box meal and shoving it into the microwave is the best Dave can expect. It's one of the few times I am grateful for plain Kibble.

CHAPTER 3

O CANADA

"I felt my lungs inflate with the onrush of scenery—air, mountains, trees, people. I thought, 'This is what it is to be happy."
                                                                    Sylvia Plath

It was only a thirty-five-mile drive from Shelby to the Canadian border. As we left Shelby, a beautiful mountain greeted us. It stood alone in the prairie, majestic and imposing. It proved to be a precursor of what was to come.

Even though Val and Dave believed they had all documents in order, there was always a slight anxiety whenever they had to prove our status. The passports were ready and my documentation from Companion Animal Hospital and Dr. Izzo were at hand. However, since Dave had a rifle, he was required to pull over and go inside to complete some paperwork.

Dave went inside while Val and I waited in the truck. Next thing we knew, Dave was back with a couple Canadian officials, and they entered the trailer. It was amazing that what took days to pack, only took these guys minutes to pull out and throw in a pile. Hours later, they decided we were legal and safe and let us go. *I'm messing with you! Dave was only inside ten minutes before we were back on the road.*

Now that we were in Canada, we had to get used to kilometers instead of miles, and liters instead of gallons. Dave said that the diesel was very expensive no matter how you measured it.

We loved the wide-open spaces. We would see cattle here and there without any sign of a barn or farmhouse as far as the eye could see, which at these heights, was quite far. Soon, we noticed herds of horses and lots of signs for horses and horse accessories. Then we saw fields of grain that went for miles with only a house here and there, to more populated farmland with more trees, and then large horse farms, to more and more populated areas. Val saw a sign designating Head-Smashed-In Buffalo Jump. *Really?* She explained that the name came from when native plains people hunted buffalo by stampeding them over a cliff, and then they harvested the buffalo on the flats at the bottom. *Ingenious for the natives, but I lost all respect for the intelligence of a buffalo. Put on the brakes, for heaven sakes!*

Before we knew it, we were in the heaviest traffic we'd encountered so far on this trip. Calgary, Alberta, is a large city, and home to the famous stampede. Dave was focused on staying in the correct lane because it takes no small effort to move from lane to lane while pulling a trailer in heavy traffic. Our knuckles turned from white to pink as we navigated away from Calgary.

As our anxiety decreased, we were rewarded with the view of snow-covered mountains in the distance, and the foreground offered a barn with a big smiley face. We began to look for a suitable place to camp for the night, hoping to find a spot near Red Deer, Alberta. But, once again, we ended up having to drive much farther before we found an open campground with no train tracks nearby. It was in Leduc.

Exhausted from a long day of travel, we ate our supper and were almost asleep before our heads hit the pillows. *Wait ... what was that? Sounds like an airplane! My goodness, it is flying very low—it's quite loud. Oh well, let's go to sleep. What's that? Another airplane.*

Wouldn't you know it, the campground was at the end of a runway. Well, if you're tired enough, you can sleep through anything. Just close your eyes, relax your body, and think good thoughts ... **Zoom! Roar!** Another plane and wide awake, again.

The next day, our goal was to reach Dawson Creek. There were no problems maneuvering around Edmonson and back into the countryside. We drove for miles without much to report on, when Val started to laugh.

"Did you see that? There was a sign that said, 'This Is A Crime Watch Area.'" Val found this humorous because we had been traveling for miles without even seeing another car—not even a crossroad for miles and miles.

Sometime later, Val said, "Dave, I have been watching as carefully as I can, and I have not seen any crime."

Dave asked, "What do you suppose crime looks like?"

She said, "As soon as I see it, I will let you know. If I see crime and call the number on the bottom of the sign, how long do you think it will take before the law gets there? One day? Two?"

While searching the horizon for crime, we saw some elk in a field. That's something to report back home.

We finally arrived at Dawson Creek—Mile 0 of the Alaska Highway, aka the Alcan. This is the road to America's Last Frontier. The road goes from Dawson Creek, British Columbia, Canada, to Delta Center, Alaska, USA—approximately 1,400 miles. The Alcan was opened to traffic in 1942, for use of and built by the military. It opened to civilian traffic after World War II. It was difficult traveling then, but the road has since been improved.

We were warned there were not many cell towers and that gas stations along the highway opened late in the morning and closed early in the day. At the visitor's center in Dawson Creek, we picked up a brochure that listed the gas stations, places to stay, and other services according to their mile marker on the highway. We highly recommend this for anyone who makes the journey.

We had a peaceful night in Dawson Creek and got up early to meet the day. We left Dawson Creek at 5:55 a.m. It was 29 degrees Fahrenheit. We saw a moose right away, at the top of a hill. That was just the beginning of a day filled with animal sightings. We saw so many animals on the stretch from Dawson Creek to Liard Hot Springs we couldn't believe it. We saw, in order, the moose, a black bear, a woodchuck, a deer, two moose headed into the bush, another deer, a black bear eating a dead moose, a live moose on the bank of the Toad River, several moose at the side of the road, six Stone sheep on the side of the road, more sheep, and a baby sheep (that would be a lamb), sheep, sheep, and a mother black bear with two cubs. My neighbor friend back home, Rudy the

Rottweiler, will never believe me when I tell him about all these critters! As often as possible, Dave would roll down my window and I was able to get both a view of these animals and an identifying smell. *Once I have a smell in my mind I never forget it. Some are more memorable than others; for example a buffalo has a more significant smell than a ground squirrel.*

What I like most are the buffalo. Woodland buffalo are seen all along the Alcan, singly and in groups. Although they are safe from cliffs here, not so much from eighteen-wheelers. I liked it when Dave slowed down or stopped so I could get my snoot full of buffalo smell. I could watch and smell them for hours, but we had a destination in mind. So, we kept on truckin'.

In addition to the animals, the scenery along this stretch was amazing. The beautiful foothills, mountains, and glacier-fed streams and rivers were spectacular for our viewing pleasure.

At Liard Hot Springs there was a wooded campground we liked. The sites are big, well-maintained, and rustic. There are two hot springs at the park. We walked on a boardwalk out to the Alpha pool. The boardwalk goes through a warm-water swamp and boreal forest. I was surprised to see fish in the swamp because the temperature of the water in the pools ranges from 108 to 126 degrees Fahrenheit. The closer to where the water enters the pool, the hotter the water.

Access to the Beta pool was closed due to bears. In 1997, a black bear killed two people at the Beta pool; so we minded the warning. And you already know how I feel about water; and I like my drinking water cold.

Although I appreciated the scents from the warm water swamp, I also enjoyed strolling through the boreal forest here. We pretty much stayed on the park roads due to the threat of black bears, but there was plenty to see and sniff as we traversed the campground. The sleeping was quiet here, but all too soon the night was over and we were back on the road.

When we drove through another time change, Dave said that gave us another hour on the road. Val said she did not understand that logic—but onward and northward we went.

The day had started out rainy, which we were grateful for because snow had been predicted. But, by the time we passed Fort St. John, which was Val's second choice for a place to stay, the rain had turned to snow. Pretty soon we were in an area where it had snowed, a lot—a foot or more. It was wet and heavy snow. However, the roads had recently been plowed and were mostly just wet.

We stopped for diesel at a place called Pink Mountain, and there was a semi-tractor pulling a travel trailer stuck in the snow near there. We were able to get in and out without getting stuck and kept heading north. Near a place called Wonowon, Val spotted a moose by the side of the road. Once again, we did not stop for me to get a sniff, so I have no idea what a moose smells like. If it's anything like a buffalo, it has a smell that is very cool.

We finally stopped for the night in Fort Nelson, British Columbia. Fort Nelson was named for the British Naval hero Horatio Nelson. It was initially a fur-trading post but is now known for its oil and gas, as well as tourism. Dave said, "Tomorrow will be only a six-hour-drive day." Let's hope. The up side of this long day was that we ended up at a nice campground with no trains and no planes.

As we set up camp, Dave talked with a man in the campground who asked if we had gone through the snowstorm in the mountains. Dave said, "I think we were behind the worst of the storm."

The man said, "That was the worst storm I have ever driven in. I was so scared. I'm from Texas and have never driven in snow like that, let alone pulling a trailer through steep hills and sharp curves. I found Jesus in those mountains!" None of us doubt that he did.

I woke up early in Fort Nelson, and I kept nudging Val until she got up and let me out. As we stepped outside, I saw something move. I went into my frozen hunting-dog stance: nose pointed toward the object, tail straight out in a line with my nose, and one paw raised—it's classic. Val looked in the direction I was looking, and there was a beautiful black dog with a big fluffy tail. Val called it a fox and ran into the trailer to get her camera. Mr. Fox was long gone by the time she got back. When he saw me, I'm sure I scared him. Everyone knows about foxes and hounds. I wish she would have just let me off that darned leash. I would have put nose to ground and found that fox again.

The Alaska Highway had taken us along the northeast corner of British Columbia into the Northern Rockies. Our next destination was Watson Lake.

"Look, there is a moose on the side of the road!" announced Dave. Once again, he is driving so fast, I miss it. And once again, no picture, and tragically, no smells. The girls back home are expecting pictures from the camera they invested in for Val, so she had better get busy.

There were lots of signs along the road warning drivers to watch for moose and buffalo. Soon we came to some buffalo by the side of the road. There was no traffic, so Dave stopped near the buffalo and rolled down my window far enough for me to get my head out and get a good sniff. I can tell you that buffalo are a whole lot bigger and smellier than my friend Rudy. I was making noises, trying to communicate with the beasts, but they would not even look my way. I couldn't tell if they were stuck up or deaf. *Wow! That was exciting!* I decided I needed to sit up in the backseat and pay attention. Maybe I would see more creatures not found back home.

You won't believe this, but soon I was standing with my feet on the center console of the truck while looking out the front window. This was a huge improvement from my lying on the backseat and throwing up—for everyone. And Val was finally taking a lot of photos. She was busy snapping pictures through the windshield. I'm no expert, but I don't think that is a technically sound picture-taking method. But every new bend in the road brought such a beautiful vista that Val could not resist. "Words are just not sufficient to describe the beauty," she said. She now really appreciated what purple mountains majesty was all about.

Our policy was to stop for fuel at every opportunity. We stopped at a place called Toad River. *Do toads live in rivers? I thought frogs lived in rivers and toads lived in trees. That is evidently not the way it works in Canada, but what do I know? I didn't do all that well in Biology 101 at Beagle University.*

Windshield View

When we saw the signpost forest, we knew we were in Watson Lake, Yukon. The signpost forest began when the Alaska Highway was being built. The people working on the project started to hang signs from their hometowns, and it continued. There were also many examples of the equipment used to build the original road.

Dave said, "Val, take some pictures of this. I think your dad would be interested in seeing this old equipment." Val's dad was in the Navy during World War II and served in Dutch Harbor, Alaska. I liked the signpost forest because it was a dog-friendly attraction. My nose told me that lots of dogs had left their marks on these signposts. Some dogs will pee on anything. Because Dave had promised us a short travel day, after visiting the signpost forest, we looked for a campground near Watson Lake.

There was only one campground open because we were traveling at the onset of the season. The Downtown RV Park in Watson Lake was basically a parking lot with hook-ups. It was fine and had lots of positives—especially if you were only staying one night. *Can you poop in a parking lot? Well, I can't either., And don't even try walking me on a leash. It just ain't gonna happen.*

The next morning, we were happy to continue our journey to the unknown. The Alcan was built with sloping banks on both sides of the road and, as we traveled, Val noticed there were words, messages,

and names written with stones in the banks. This "stone graffiti" appeared to be a cultural phenomenon that continued for hundreds of kilometers. Unlike other types of graffiti, stone graffiti does not contain any dirty words, as far as we could tell.

The scenery on the way from Watson Lake to Whitehorse, Yukon, was mountainous and gorgeous. When we reached the Continental Divide, the odometer told us we had gone 217 miles since Liard. From this point, the rivers would flow north.

Teslin, Yukon, Canada

Val said that, in her opinion, one of the prettiest places on the planet was a little community called Teslin, on the banks of Teslin Lake. We stopped on the crest of a hill just for the view. Teslin Lake looked like a river as it curved around the jutting peninsula, and the blue and white of the mountains in the distance were the crowning glory. Earth tones of green and brown from the boreal forest blended together and ended at the water's edge. The bridge, however, was not aesthetic, but it was functional and we are grateful for the easy access to the town and the continuing highway.

The Hudson's Bay Company established a trading post in Teslin long before the Alaska Highway was even thought of. The name *Teslin* comes from a Tlingit word, *Teslintoo*. Teslin has a large population of First Nation Teslin Inland Tlingit. If you travel this way, don't miss the George Johnston Museum for some local history.

The George Johnston Museum showcases the story of how the inland Tlingits made their way from Juneau to Teslin in the early twentieth century. They came to this area to trap, and then would return to Juneau to sell their furs. Eventually the fur buyers came to them to bid on the furs. George Johnston was a self-taught Tlingit photographer who recorded the early culture of the people in this area. He believed it was important to preserve the Tlingit traditions and history. He brought the first car to Teslin, even though there were no roads yet. George and his friends built some roads to drive the car on, and that stretch was later integrated into the Alaska Highway.

In 1942, life for the Tlingit changed dramatically when the highway cut through their village. They did not protest because they believed the road was vital for the U.S. war effort. Unfortunately, soldiers and road-construction workers brought sickness, measles and chickenpox, that the natives were susceptible to. Many people died. And, to add insult to injury, the U.S. military decided the Tlingit looked too much like Japanese, so the natives were issued identification, which they had to show as they traveled the highway— on land that was theirs alone before the invasion of the U.S. military.

There was a nice campground in Teslin, at the base of the bridge. Val loved this place because it was located on the lake, with a gas station, motel, gift shop, and restaurant. A restaurant close to a campground was a treat because when we traveled, we only unhooked the trailer from the truck when we had to. Dave and Val could walk to the restaurant and bring me some leftovers. I was very happy because I was getting tired of plain Kibble.

The bonus was sitting outside after dinner to enjoy the beautiful lake view. When Val commented that I didn't appreciate how lucky I was, I ignored her. That was not true. When I am with my humans, I always feel loved and safe.

Although we didn't want to leave Teslin, we had to stay focused on our final destination: Denali Park. Our next stop for the night was in Whitehorse, still in the Yukon Territory. Whitehorse provided us with our first view of the Yukon River. The Yukon River begins its journey in British Columbia and slithers back and forth all the way to the Bering Sea. *Wow!* The city was named for the rapids, which are called White Horse because they look like the mane of a white horse. Whitehorse was on a route used by gold stampeders traveling by river in the 1890's.

I have to say that the campground in Whitehorse, Hi Country, was top-of-the-line. Dave had to pay for our stay with a credit card. When he explained to the lady that we had spent all the Canadian cash we had exchanged U.S. dollars for when we first entered the country, she asked, "Did you come through British Columbia?"

Dave said, "Yes—part of the way."

She said, "That explains why you ran out of money. Most people think BC means British Columbia, but it actually stands for Bring Cash."

Whitehorse Campground has lovely wooded lots, no trains, no planes, lots of smells, and many places to go—well, you know. The doggy potty walk is a plus, and I was so relieved—literally. When we got back from the potty walk, Dave was grilling steaks. Unfortunately, there were only two steaks on that grill. One for me, one for Dave ... I wondered what Val was going to eat. As it ended up, Val and Dave ate steak, and I had Kibble. *How rude!*

Yukon River at Whitehorse

Seven o'clock in the morning found the three of us back on the road. Our next destination was Tok, Alaska, USA. Although it was not a sunny day and we had driven through sporadic rain showers, the views were fabulous. Val was snapping pictures through the windshield again. If Dave stopped the truck every time Val wanted a picture, we would never make it to Denali Park in time to start our jobs as campground hosts.

After stopping for fuel in Haines Junction, the highway took us around a very big lake. No matter how you say Kluane, it is absolutely beautiful. The Alcan cut into the mountainside around the edge of Kluane Lake. There was some major road construction going on in this area, so much of the road was gravel. As Dave slowly drove through the construction zone, we had the opportunity to look for mountain sheep. We saw some, and shot all of them—with a camera of course. But the sheep were so far away they looked like pieces of rice on green paper.

What's happening up ahead? There were several vehicles pulled off of the road. As we got closer, I could see that people were out of their cars and trucks, holding cameras and binoculars. *Must be something here to see … Yikes! A brown bear—a grizzly!* Val hopped out and tried to get close enough to the bear to get a picture while staying close enough to the truck to escape the bear if it headed toward her. *Wow! That was exciting!* That'll get the fur standing straight up on your back. We were so far away that, although I could get a slight smell, I could only see it when it moved. The humans definitely had more grizzly fun than I did that day.

Our first grizzly in the wild!

Traveling on this part of the Alaska Highway was like riding waves. We rode the road up, and then **Boom!**, the road was gone from under us and we came down. I decided to curl up on the backseat and try not to be sick.

The road would get a little better for a while, and then back to a patch of undulating blacktop. Wherever the road was especially bad, there were orange flags on sticks alongside the shoulder. Evidently, this roller-coaster effect was caused from the original road being constructed over permafrost. Enough of the dirt over the permafrost was removed when the road was installed, and so now, when the permafrost warms from the heat of the road, it eventually melts and the road sinks. I wonder if the road will improve when we cross into Alaska and the USA?

CHAPTER 4

BACK IN THE GOOD OLE' USA

"I'm a storyteller; that's what exploration really is all about.
Going to places where others haven't been and returning to tell
a story they haven't heard before."   James Cameron

The U.S. Border Guards were a piece of cake. They didn't ask much. I think it was because they were so taken with me. One of them said, "Oh, a beagle. I just love beagles." *Well, who doesn't?* Another one gave me a cookie. Soon we were on our way, proving that a beagle is a handy gadget for passing through customs.

When we crossed the border, in anticipation that the road would improve once we were in Alaska, we felt like celebrating. Unfortunately, the road was not any better for the rest of the drive to Tok, Alaska. In spite of the undulating road distracting us, we saw a picnic table and next to it one of those cutout black bears people use as lawn ornaments. *Yikes! It's not a cutout bear—it's the real thing!* It turned and ran off before I could get a good sniff.

Just as we were calming down from the excitement of a close encounter with a black bear, we saw the sign for our campground. The campground in Tok was the kind we like. It had some trees and pull-through sites so we didn't have to unhook the trailer. It's a good thing the parking was easy because when Val opened the door to the trailer it looked like a giant monster had picked up the trailer and shaken it like a big salt shaker before putting it back down. The cupboards were open, the table was tipped over, chairs, dishes, and canned goods were all over the place. Some things were broken, including the glass tray for the microwave.

Although I was getting pretty good at human speak, Val said some words that I had not heard before. I sense they were not nice. My plan was to just stay out of her way until she was in a better frame of mind. Fortunately for all of us, the mess was cleaned up quickly. I was taken for a walk and some potty privacy; then we hurried back to the trailer.

Because Val had been talking about the Top of the World Highway and Dawson City, Yukon, for a long time, we decided to take a day to see what we could find. Chicken, Alaska, was on the way from Tok to Dawson City. As luck would have it, we arrived in Chicken during a music festival. *You've heard of Woodstock? Well, this was Chickenstock!*

We saw two World War II-era trucks backed up to each other; the stage was the flatbeds of the trucks. The place was crawling with old people trying their best to retain their status as hippies, and young people who, I guessed, were wannabe hippies trying to recreate days gone by. Val said she hadn't seen that many tie-dyed shirts in years. The music wasn't identifiable as bluegrass, country, jazz, or rock and roll. Actually, Dave and Val didn't recognize one song.

One end of town was occupied by a lot of high-end motor coaches, and the opposite end was full of tents. A vivid separation between the high-class former hippies and the nature lovers. We walked around the gold dredge for a while. Dave tried panning for gold without luck. I was not enthused because the smells were mostly bird feathers and poop, mixed with a little domesticated doggie doo. The doggie doo was, for the most part, Purina; I was not impressed. The gift shop offered items from Chicken University, such as lapel pins that said "Go Peckers." You gotta love it. I didn't want to point any fingers at the festival guests, but the air had a tang to it I couldn't recognize.

Time to return to our truck and be on our way to Dawson. At least we could listen to music we recognized. You can't beat "On The Road Again" by Willie Nelson for a traveling tune.

The Top of the World Highway between Chicken and the Canadian border was not good road. It was dirt, and not much more than a two-track in most places. We saw gold miners along the way. Some had small dredges, and some were panning. We would have loved to stop and try our luck, but this was not a recreational mining area. These were legal claims, and we did not want to get shot at for some flakes of gold.

Once we crossed the border into Canada, the road improved dramatically. A lot of it was paved, which was a good thing because we were traveling above the tree line. The elevation at the border was 4,127 feet, but I don't think that was the highest elevation along this route.

When we reached the Yukon River, we had to wait for the ferry to cross over to Dawson. Once across, we admired the old town and its wooden boardwalks and history oozing out of every building. Dawson was not a metropolis, but it was easy to imagine the place swarming with prospectors. It took a great deal of stamina and perseverance just to get here in the 1890s. And some pretty interesting characters were known to have lived here. We found the Robert Service log cabin, and Jack London's former residence. My favorite Jack London novels are, of course, *White Fang* and *Call of the Wild*. I admire the dogs in these novels for their struggles and victories against their environment and other animals. *I know that given the opportunity I could do those same feats of bravery – in my dreams I am often a hero.* Val said she admires both of these artists and would like to spend a summer in Dawson, just soaking up the writing atmosphere. Unfortunately spending the summer was not an option so instead we shopped at a hardware store where Val bought an old basket, and then Dave spent considerably more at a gold exchange where he bought a gold nugget.

Because the border was only open from 9 am to 7 pm PST, we decided to head back. If you get to the border after seven and it is closed, you must wait until the next morning for it to open again. Dave asked the border guard if he was assigned to this outpost as a punishment for bad behavior. The guard assured Dave that was not the case, and that many people ask to be assigned there. The vegetation is sparse due to the high elevations, and the landscape appears pretty barren, but there is plenty to do during hours off of work.

The next morning, after leaving Tok, our first stop was Delta Junction, Alaska. Delta Junction was the end of the Alaska Highway. We stopped at the Visitor's Center where there was a large sculpture of a mosquito. Dave and Val insisted that I pose for a picture that looks like I am being bitten by this monster mosquito. They thought it was extremely funny. Val showed the camera screen to Dave and he laughed. I realized it will be some time before I understand their humor. *Oh, the things I do for these humans.*

The community of North Pole, Alaska, draws many tourists based on its name. Businesses and government entities were happy to help by using Christmas and Santa themes. The streetlights looked like candy canes and the post office was enhanced with candy canes as well. There was a large gift shop where you could sit on Santa's lap and look for gifts for those back home. Santa has some of his reindeer in a pen near the gift shop. I tried to communicate because Val wanted to know which one was Dancer, Prancer, Donner and Blitzen, but they did not want to reveal their secrets to me. There was absolutely no sign of Rudolph.

From North Pole, the road took us north in a highway parabola that would take us back south after passing through Fairbanks. We traveled south from Fairbanks on the highway that was the main access to Denali National Park and Preserve. The highway, referred to as Parks Highway, was not named for the park it gives access to. The highway was named for George Parks, who was territorial governor of Alaska from 1925 to 1933. Beyond Denali Park, the highway primarily follows the railroad all the way to Anchorage, many miles away. Parks Highway took us through some small communities; Nenana is one we knew we would revisit during our stay. Once we passed Healy, we knew we were near our destination.

CHAPTER 5

OUR NEW ADDRESS

"Heaven is under our feet as well as over our heads."
Henry David Thoreau

The Parks Highway winds through the seasonal community of Denali Park. It is abutted on one side by the Nenana River, and on the other side of the Parks Highway the town is tucked into the mountainside. Tourist season would begin soon, and we saw store owners receiving orders from shippers and setting up their shops. This tourist town consisted of several nice hotels, some restaurants, one gas station/party store, and many gift shops. Some call it "glitter gulch," but Park Service personnel correct that terminology to "the canyon." The town was well-planned and designed. -Everything was built with log construction or at least had a rustic look.

Denali Park

I could feel the anticipation as the truck turned off of the Parks Highway into Denali National Park and Preserve. Dogs easily pick up on the emotion of their humans. Val admitted that her thoughts were somewhat fearful, she was a city girl after all. In contrast, Dave was the confident outdoorsman and right in his element. As hosts, we arrived before the start of the season, but there were some hardy campers already there.

Riley Creek was the first campground we found inside the park, and it is the largest. Open year-round, it only charges fees for camping during the summer. The Mercantile, located in Riley Creek, offered showers; a laundry; and a gift shop with limited groceries and, most importantly, ice cream. Riley Creek was close to the Visitor's Center, the Wilderness Access Center, and the town of Denali Park. The Visitor's Center provided educational programs and entertainment; and the Wilderness Access Center is where you signed up for bus rides and tours. The town offered additional shopping opportunities.

We set up camp in Riley Creek, to await the opening of our assigned location in Savage River Campground, where we would work as camp hosts.

Prior to the start of the season, visitors were allowed to drive into the park as far as Teklanika Campground. Usually tourists can only travel by car as far as the Savage River checkpoint, just a mile or so past Savage River Campground, located approximately thirteen miles into the park. Teklanika is farther out, at approximately mile thirty of the park road. We made the journey; Dave drove slowly, hoping to see wildlife. I was on alert with my front paws on the console, wagging my tail in anticipation. It was not long before I was rewarded.

Two beautiful, large wolves were calmly walking alongside the road; they did not seem the least concerned when we stopped to take their pictures. Later we learned that the male wolf had been snared outside of the park. The snare around his neck wore the fur and skin right off. He made it back to the park with the snare still attached. Typically, park rangers do not interfere with life-and-death issues concerning the animals, but because the injury to this wolf was manmade, they darted the wolf with a tranquilizer and removed the snare. The officials told us that a big factor in his survival was that his mate licked his wound, keeping it clean until it healed. *Of course, she did.* Licking a wound comes naturally to a canine, sometimes to the point of not being helpful, which is why you will sometimes see a dog with a plastic cone around his/her neck to restrict those desires. In fact, we are not particular in our licking, and will even lick the wounds of humans. Humans don't get it; they think it's yucky. They need a conversation with this wolf whose life was saved by his licking mate.

Not as exciting as spotting the wolves, we noticed pieces of snowshoe hare along the roadside and even in the trees. Apparently, snowshoe hares are in the basic food group of the carnivores that live here—and none like to eat the feet of the hare. From the viewpoint of the snowshoe, it must suck to be at the bottom of the food chain. I wouldn't want to eat a hare because I prefer my Kibble, but I wouldn't mind chasing and catching one! Although wolves are among the "Big Five" animals to see in the park, the snowshoe is significant due to its numbers among the small animals that live in the park.

Snowshoe Hare

We couldn't believe our eyes when we spotted a lynx. The snowshoe hare and lynx are connected in a boom-and-bust cycle of about eight to eleven years. When snowshoe hares reach a climax in population, lynx and fox also increase in number. When the snowshoes are depleted, the number of lynx and fox goes down. Since the snowshoe hare were at or near the high point in population at the time, so were the lynx. *Great looking cat, but what happened to his tail? From the look on his face it seems that he has an attitude. Well, I would probably have an attitude, too, if someone took my tail.*

Ptarmigan were also prevalent. Ptarmigan are pure white in the winter and turn to mottled brown in the summer, much like grouse. I wouldn't mind catching one of the birds. I would eat it too, if someone would get rid of the feathers and the innards. I bet it would be good grilled, maybe with some wild rice. I would just sneak up, ever so carefully and pounce! That would be my plan if I was let loose from the truck.

We were looking for a moose, but instead we saw caribou. In early summer, they don't have big antlers. We learned that the main difference between caribou and reindeer is that the reindeer are domesticated and caribou are wild. And, of course, reindeer can fly.

We had already seen more animals in one day than we ever expected to see. *Wow! This is some cool place.*

We located our work site, but we couldn't get in because there was a locked gate. Savage River Campground was located 12.8 miles out on the park road, and the elevation was 2,780 feet above sea level. The main camp at Riley Creek is about 1,000 feet lower in elevation.

There was taiga and tundra visible from the park road. *Taiga* means evergreen forest in Russian, and *tundra* is the area above the tree line. Here, the taiga was mostly black spruce with straight, tall, skinny, trunks and short, spindly branches. Aspen, birch, and poplar were also part of the taiga, but looked more like bushes than trees because of the higher elevation.

The tundra could either be moist or dry. The moist tundra was covered with moss and lichens; it felt like walking on sponges. Dry tundra was like walking on rock. This difference made hiking interesting because one moment you would be on dry tundra, and in the next step you could be up to your knees in moist tundra.

We had been promised a generator to power our trailer, but because we had not actually started to work yet, we didn't have it and the trailer's batteries were draining fast. On morning two, we woke up cold in Riley Creek Campground. However, on the way to the SST (sweet-smelling toilet) Val saw a person sleeping on the ground in a mummy sack sleeping bag covered with snow. She said that sight made her feel like a wimp.

The problem with no power was not going to improve, and there were several more days before we would be starting our assignment. We never thought we would long for the sound of a train whistle or low-flying airplanes—but those places did have power hook-ups and we were warm there.

The generator we were eventually provided by our employer was a disappointment because it was not big enough to power the trailer. It could not fully charge the trailer's batteries during the hours we were allowed to run the generator; so, it got very cold in the trailer when the batteries died each night—in the middle of the night.

This necessitated a 100-mile trip to Fairbanks for some new batteries. After we got the new batteries, we had enough power to get us through the night by running the generator to charge the batteries during the allowable hours for generator operation. We did not use our precious power for anything except the blower on the furnace.

It got cold at night—usually in the thirties. And it was true, we were wimps. There was a lovely little doggy bed in the bedroom of the trailer that started out to be my sleeping space, but body heat is a wonderful thing to share. I found that in the middle of the night I could ease my way onto Dave and Val's bed, and snuggle between them for some added warmth. They never said anything or pushed me off, so it wasn't long before I just jumped up there when we first went to bed. They did get a bit possessive of their space when, from the middle of the bed, I pushed them toward the edge. That struggle continues to this day.

In between orientation sessions, the three of us spent our time learning about our new environment. We took a short hike to Horseshoe Lake, and I loved it. The trail was marked, but it was full of tree roots, zigs and zags, ups and downs. My nose was in overdrive with the fragrant smell of snowshoe hare, ground squirrels, and ptarmigan. *Wait! What is that smell? Is it buffalo? No. Let's see ... maybe it's a moose. I never smelled a moose before.* Sniff, sniff. *Yeah, I think it could be moose.*

On our way back to the truck, Dave and Val saw a sign that said it was against the rules to walk a dog on the trails. I'm glad they didn't read it on the way to Horseshoe Lake, but sad because I was now eliminated from off-road hikes. *Maybe they didn't mean beagles. Especially well-mannered ones like me ...*

One morning, as we were driving out of Riley Creek Campground, we heard people exclaiming, "Oh, my gosh! It's a moose! A mother moose and a baby moose!" Campers and other campground hosts were taking pictures of the moose; the animals seemed oblivious to the attention. I was shaking and whimpering. I wanted to get out of the truck and get at it so bad, I just couldn't stand it. The mother moose was huge. I think she was taller than a buffalo. And from the window of the truck, I can say that her smell was unique—not at all like a buffalo.

Mother Moose

Baby Moose

While still waiting for assignment to Savage Campground, Dave and Val were invited to "Cabin Night," a dinner theatre in Denali Park. The theme for the event was the Gold Rush days in Alaska. Guests sit at picnic tables and the food is served family-style. Val reported that the food was good, but the entertainment was better. The actors entice people from the audience to participate, and Dave was pulled out of the crowd to play the part of the old prospector. His co-actors whispered the lines in his ear, and then he would say the lines. Val said she laughed so hard she was crying.

While we were at Riley Creek Campground, waiting for Savage River Campground to open, we took long walks through Riley Creek and got tips on how to be campground hosts from Carole and Larry. I was uniquely qualified as a campground host because I communicate a welcoming atmosphere by being cute and wagging my tail—with people and dogs and other animals.

Moose were plentiful at Riley Creek, and I must admit they didn't seem to notice my cute tail wagging. Now, maybe

Dave as the Old Prospector

if Dave and Val would have let me get closer to the moose, they would see how adorable I was and would want to make friends. The moose came into the campground at Riley Creek because they were safer there from wolves and bear. The females came into the park to have their young. (A camper told us about a video he took of a big grizzly bear attacking a mother moose in order to kill and eat her baby.) We saw a big cow moose with a collar, and her calf from last year. We also saw two young moose with no mothers wandering around.

One day as Val and Dave left the dining hall, they spotted two moose. The rules were to keep your distance from moose. More people are injured by moose in the park than by grizzly bears. The moose will charge and trample people. We were taught that if a moose is charging, you should run and try to hide behind trees. The moose are so big it is hard for them to maneuver in the trees and they give up.

I had a picture in my mind of Dave and Val dodging between trees with me on a leash. It was not a pretty image. Although I would love to butt sniff a moose, I am glad that I am kept on an enforced distance from them. Besides, I would need a ladder to reach high enough for a smell. Even though they are homely looking animals, they are so huge and powerful they have my respect.

Dave was making chili one night for all of the hosts. It smelled so good; I would have loved to have some, but once again, the humans got the good stuff and I got Kibble. The human gathering was fun though. After the chili supper, entertainment was provided by a bus driver named Monte Carpenter. He played the guitar and sang to us, and with us. Monte sang such classics as "Home Grown Tamatas," and "I Just Don't Look Good Naked Anymore." Val loves his CD. I enjoyed singing, but I had a hard time with melody. I must have been off-key because people kept shushing me.

My favorite person of the group was Carole. She liked me. I could tell because she talked baby talk to me and scratched my ears. Carole and Larry used to have a beagle that they loved. Val said she understands why Carole loves me. She loves me because I am so special; I'm like the cream in her coffee.

Monte the singing bus driver.

CHAPTER 6

LIVING AND WORKING
AT SAVAGE RIVER

"Something will have gone out of us as a people if we ever let the remaining wilderness be destroyed ... We need wilderness preserved—as much of it as is still left, and as many kinds— because it was the challenge against which our character as a people was formed."   *Wallace Stegner*

It was moving day! We were finally setting up our camp in Savage River Campground. We walked the whole campground and made a map of all the campsites, the water access points, the SSTs (sweet-smelling toilets) and the flush-toilet buildings. The flush toilets were not operational because we did not yet have water.

The park staff was working on getting us water, but it was only May 18, and the ground was still frozen. We were told it would be awhile before we would have water at Savage River. According to park management, this is the interior of Alaska, and no one should expect running water or any other convenience for that matter. Our option was to drive to Healy and fill water containers there. Since Healy was twenty-six miles from Savage Campground, we learned to use our water sparingly. I do have to admit that I love bottled water in my doggy dish.

Because May 19 was the last day private vehicles would be allowed to go as far as Teklanika, we decided to take another road trip into the park. We stopped at the Sanctuary River Camp, and Dave tried fishing—with no luck. While Dave played in the water, Val and I just wandered around, soaking up the pristine beauty. There is nothing like a walk in a boreal forest with the sound of rushing water from the river nearby.

We did not see another human while we were there, and other than some little squirrels, we saw no animals. I am more into the smells than the sights, but we both enjoyed our walk. On the drive back to Savage River Campground, we saw some grizzly bears. They were quite far from the road, and therefore not much in the way of smells, but Val managed to get a picture.

Campground hosts are trained for bear encounters. The first rule was that you never run from a grizzly. They can run faster than a human or a beagle, and if you run the bear will view you as prey. If you see a bear, and the bear does not see you, the thing to do is to put distance between yourself and the bear. If the bear sees you, slowly raise your arms in order to appear larger than the bear and slowly back away. You should talk in a low voice to the bear because Denali bears are not familiar with the human voice. It is suggested that you repeat, "Hey, bear. Hey, bear. Hey, bear." Most times the bear will go in the opposite direction. If it does not leave and instead heads toward you, keep up the dialog, and do not drop into the fetal position with your arms over your head unless they actually make contact with you. Sometimes they will lunge and grunt at you and then leave you alone. If you drop into a fetal position too soon they are curious and will possibly bat you around a bit before leaving. The batting around can prove to be quite painful, we were told. However, we were encouraged to learn that there has never been a fatality in the park due to a bear attack. (That changed in later years. A photographer was attacked and killed, perhaps because he got too close.)

The three of us were finally settled in at Savage River Campground. When I say "settled in" that means we had a wonderful campsite in one of the most beautiful spots in the world. We were near enough to the Savage River to hear it as it sped north into the park, and we were surrounded by mountains. There was still no running water and no power other than a pathetically inefficient generator, but we were excited to be here and the inconveniences seemed minor.

Val was happy to stay close to camp for a while. Near the trailer, she snapped a picture of a sweet little bird she later identified from the bird book as a Yellow-rumped Warbler.

The next bird she saw was a Ptarmigan that was molting from white to brown.

It seems that every day there was a reason to jump in the truck and head into the main camp at Riley Creek. I was getting so good at riding in the truck, that when Dave said, "Let's go for a ride" I would run out and wait for him to open the back door so I could hop in and get perched on the console.

I was able to see so much from up there, like the huge rocks called *erratics*. An erratic is a piece of rock that "deviates from the size and type of rock native to the area in which it rests" according to the internet. Landslides or rock falls initially dropped the rocks on top of glacial ice. The glaciers moved, taking the rocks with them. When the ice melted, the rocks were left. If you look at the picture below, you will see a dark shape above and slightly to the right of the middle pine tree in the foreground. That is an erratic. We were told that it was as big as a two-story house. *WOW!*

Do you see the erratic?

The campground was full over Memorial Day weekend. The number of hikers staying in tents was surprising. There were also lots of c-class RVs that people coming off of the cruise ships and airplanes rented in Anchorage and drove north to get a peek at the interior of Alaska.

The park had three group campsites, and one of these sites was occupied by a wilderness tour. The tour company came in and set up tents for their guests, and they provided meals out of a chuck wagon trailer. Excitement for the weekend was provided by two grizzly-bear sightings on Sunday. One was at the far end of the campground near the river, and the other one was at the gate to the old campground.

Before the day ended, we met Mr. and Mrs. Howard from Michigan. Their attraction to our campfire was none other than—you guessed it—Remington Beagle. They said they thought I was bigger than a beagle should be, but Val explained, "Remington is a fourteen-inch beagle. There are also twelve-inch beagles." In spite of my size, the Howards petted me and stroked my ears. They adored me. Mrs. Howard said,

"Why don't you give Remington to us, and you can go back to your breeder and get another one?" Of course, Val and Dave declined. They would never part with such a wonderful companion as me. Val said, "No. Remington Beagle is the French fries in my Happy Meal."

As the crow flies, Savage River is not far from where Christopher McCandless lived and died in the school bus. The book *Into the Wild* is a story about Christopher and his fascination for living in the wilderness. A local man picked Christopher up when he was hitchhiking on the Park Highway and dropped him off at Stampede Road. Christopher hiked out the Stampede Road and into the wilderness. Much later, he was found deceased in a school bus by some hikers.

After reading the book, Dave and Val decided to have a look at Stampede Road and its surroundings. The end of the road, near the Park Highway, had some homes and rustic resorts, but soon the terrain opened up to rolling hills and the road disintegrated to a two-track. As the road got rougher and rougher, we stopped and walked around a bit. Dave did not want to get the truck stuck in the wilderness. I loved it because it gave me a chance to "go to ground" and do some serious sniffing. Val reminisced about a quote from Christopher McCandless: "The joy of life comes from our encounters with new experiences, and hence there is no greater joy than to have an endlessly changing horizon, for each day to have a new and different sun."

On the occasion of our first trip out Stampede Road, this had special meaning for us. Rest in peace, Christopher.

CHAPTER 7

FISHING IN FERRY AND HOMER

"All Americans believe that they are born fisherman. For a man to admit a distaste for fishing would be like denouncing mother-love or hating moonlight."
                                                    John Steinbeck

In addition to tourists, we struck up a friendship with an interesting fellow from the cleaning team. Foster was a veritable encyclopedia of information on the area. He had hiked most of the park, and even attempted a summit of McKinley some years back. Foster told Dave where the original Savage River Camp was located, and Dave found some old bottles and a broken dish at the designated spot.

Our co-worker, mountain climber, and mountain man Foster directed Dave to a fishing spot near where he lived. He said: "Take the Parks Highway north to Ferry Road." It was not very far on Ferry Road when we started seeing No Trespassing signs. Dave kept driving, of course, and soon we saw the spot where Foster said everyone parks. There was a railroad grade and bridge with more signs that said Keep Out—This Means You! Dave parked the truck in the parking lot, which could also pass for a junkyard because it appeared that many of the vehicles had not been driven in quite a while.

Dave was excited about going fishing. He busied himself getting his gear ready. "Want to come fishing with me?"

"No, Dave. I'll just sit here with the dog and wait for the police to come and arrest me for trespassing."

Dave shrugged and headed down the railroad tracks, as happy as if he was in his right mind. I took a nap while Val wrote some notes and read a book. Just when we thought maybe Dave had gotten lost or eaten by a bear, he appeared. "Get the camera out!" he shouted. "I've got some fish!"

He did get some fish—seven nice Grayling. Grayling used to be found in Michigan long ago, but they are now extinct there. They have a distinctive dorsal fin and are known to be very good eating. Thankfully, the Arctic Grayling are still plentiful in Alaska.

Carpe Diem does not mean fish of the day! Unknown Author

Ferry, Alaska, a one-of-a-kind place, was located across the river about a quarter of a mile. Getting there entails crossing the river on the railroad bridge. Thankfully there is a pedestrian part of the bridge next to the train tracks. The Alaska Railroad runs trains past the sign for Ferry; it used to be a stop on the line. Ferry even had its own post office. The post office building was still there, but it was privately owned.

DeVere Pieschl greeted us and gave us a tour of the town. He had a baby grand piano in his living room and a hard-wired telephone. Every year he hosted a solstice party, and when the train comes through, his guests moon the train. They have been doing it for so long that it had become tradition and the train now slowed down for the spectacle. DeVere gave us one of his business cards, but we were not sure what his business is—mayor of Ferry?

We were invited to Homer, Alaska, to go fishing with Tracy and Ron Palm, the aunt and uncle of our son-in-law Luke Reynolds. After a brief stop in Anchorage, we headed for the Kenai Peninsula and our destination.

The trip out of Anchorage was incredible. As we drove south, the road twisted and turned between water on the right and mountains on the left. Still visible on the mountainsides were drill marks from when workers blasted away the mountain to make the road. A road sign told us we were in Chugach State Park; looking at the water side of the road, it was evident that it was not high tide. The sea had receded, leaving some puddles, sandbars, and driftwood.

Although it was totally overcast, with a misty rain coming down, it was a beautiful sight. We traveled along the road that ran parallel with the water, or where the water had been, in a valley with mountains on both sides. What a truly spectacular sight. The tops of the mountains were snow-covered, but as the eye traveled from the mountain top to the valley, the white snow turned to gray, then black and brown tundra, then to lush green. There were sporadic little waterfalls of snowmelt run-off spurting out through the green foliage and out of the rock face. It was take-your-breath-away gorgeous.

Just past the sign for Girdwood, the inlet we had been following disappeared into wetlands and the road left the valley floor to twist and turn through rolling hills and riverbanks.

The color of the river water was noticeable because it was a bright turquoise. The water was fast moving over rocky river bottoms. As the water splashed over rocky rapids, it was cloudy and the color went from deep turquoise at the deepest points to a lighter green and then to white bubbly flumes of spray. This beautiful water contrasted with the dark-green and black of the predominant Black Spruce forest abutting the riverbank. Occasional lighter green leafy undergrowth blended into this exquisite scenery. *I must acknowledge that I know water does not have a color. It just appears to have color due to reflections from the sky and other influences.*

When we came to the Russian River, we saw that these beautiful rivers were more than just scenery. There were hundreds of fishermen lined along the river's bank and wading in the water in hopes of catching a salmon. It occurred to me that the grizzly bears were also in competition for the salmon. I would not want to be a lone fisherman here, but I guess there was safety in numbers.

Soon we were on higher ground and overlooking Cook Inlet. From this height, the road revealed snow-covered volcanoes on the other side of the inlet many, many miles away. One of the volcanoes appeared to be smoking—or maybe it was just cloud cover. Before we knew it, we were coming down a hillside and we could see Homer ahead of us.

Homer Spit

Homer was situated on a spit that went several miles into Cook Inlet. As we drove onto the spit to find our campground, Dave said, "The spit was pretty much wiped out and under water after the 1964 earthquake and the tsunami that followed." *Gosh, I hope there are no earthquakes this weekend!* Our campground, The Homer Spit Campground, was out very near the end of the spit. The campsite was not many feet from the water of Cook Inlet.

While Dave and Val set up the camp, we saw a bald eagle on the beach in front of the campsite. I wanted to go over and say hi, but Dave held me back and Val took pictures. As we looked around, we saw a few more eagles along the shore. We learned that we were camped just a few sites down from a woman who feeds the eagles in the winter. Her name was Jean Keene and she is also known as the Eagle Lady. In Cary Anderson's book, *The Eagle Lady*, we learned that Jean was originally from the lower forty-eight and came to Alaska in the 1970s. She drove to Alaska from Minnesota in the motorhome we saw not far from where we were camped. She started feeding two eagles on the beach outside her motorhome, and in a few short years she was hauling barrels of fish heads and freezer-burned fish every day to supply food for about 300 eagles. It takes her about an hour to throw the fish heads and pieces of fish to eagles perched on top of her motorhome, on pieces of driftwood on the beach, and on the hood of her pickup. She has rescued injured eagles and taken them to a veterinarian in Anchorage. Jean Keene's care of the eagles of Kachemak Bay is part of the unique history of Homer.

The next thing I knew, Dave and Val locked me up in the trailer and took off for an adventure without me. It was late in the day when they left, nearly past their bedtime. What were they thinking? It was even later, or should I say earlier the next day, before they returned. They were talking about what a good time they had catching fish. Evidently, Val caught the first fish, and Eric caught the second fish, and what great people Ron and Tracy are—amazing and wonderful people. Val and Dave dropped into bed in short order and it was quiet for several hours.

When the alarm clock went off, I couldn't believe it! This was very early for us to be up. I had my paws crossed that I would get to go with them. As soon as Dave picked up my leash, I knew I was included. *Woot woot!*

We went down the road a short way in the truck and Dave parked it in front of a big hole in the ground filled with water and boats. The hole in the ground was a marina, and this marina was floating. The docks were cement on top of Styrofoam and were connected to metal pilings with rings so that they rose and fell with the tide. The ramp that connected the docks to the land also rose and fell with the tide, so that at high tide there was a slight slope down to the docks, but at low tide—put on your brakes and hang on! It was steep going down, and if you needed to go up with a cart full of fish, better bring your muscles. Dave and Val must be nuts if they thought I was going to walk down a metal grating toward that water. But, before I knew what was happening, I was walking headfirst into the water-filled pit! I went tenaciously down that grating, and I didn't like it one bit. The docks were okay—actually I couldn't even tell they were floating when I walked on them. But, going from the dock to the boat was another story.

The boat was the *Courtney Rose,* and she was beautiful with twin Honda 225 outboard motors. Captain Ron guided the *Courtney Rose* through the marina and out into Cook Inlet to his favorite fishing spot. It was a pretty calm day; none of us got seasick. I was busy sniffing all over the boat, and when the first Halibut was caught I couldn't believe it. I had never seen anything like this in my life. It was brown on one side and white on the other. It had two buggy eyes on the brown side. It was wet and slippery and smelled like a fish.

Ron, Tracy, Eric, Dave, and Val were limited to two halibut each, and the limit was caught in about an hour and a half. Since we had a full day ahead of us, we decided to go to Seldovia for lunch.

The Courtney Rose at Seldovia

Seldovia was a quaint little fishing village on the opposite shore of Cook Inlet from Homer. You can only get there by boat or plane. I got to go along with the gang into town. They found a nice restaurant with a deck. The original plan was to eat outside on the deck, but it was too cold, so I waited out on the deck while the people went inside the restaurant to eat. It was okay with me because I could see them from where I was on the deck, and I was confident that I would be rewarded when they finished.

After lunch we walked around town for a while. One of the town residents was a wood sculptor. Examples of his skill can be found around town.

When we returned to the boat, the guys loaded our fish into a cart and hauled them off to the cleaning table. I got left on the boat with Tracy while Val and the guys went to clean fish. I didn't like being left behind. I am nosey and wanted to know what was going on, so I jumped out of the boat and met up with the gang at the fish-cleaning station. Boy, were they surprised to see me. They had lined up the day's catch on the table for a picture. Halibut sure are ugly. Their eyes start out one on each side of their heads, but then they move (it's called *eye migration*) so both eyes end up on the brown side. Amazing. I don't mind *migrating*, but leave my eyes alone.

When the fish were cleaned, the people loaded them into coolers, and after storing them on the boat, we fired up the *Courtney Rose* and headed back to Homer. On the way, Tracy cooked some halibut on the boat. The folks ate first, but they did save me some scraps, and boy it was good. That was what fresh fish tasted like!

Back on shore and at our campsite, it was okay with me to be left in the trailer because I was exhausted. Dave and Val took off to meet Ron, Tracy, and Eric at a restaurant called Land's End, and it was at land's end. According to Val, the food was superb and the view even better. From Land's End they went to the Salty Dog, a very old landmark bar on the spit. It survived the '64 tsunami even though it was underwater. The ceilings were low and every available inch of wall space was covered with signed dollar bills. Everyone got a t-shirt from the Salty Dog—except the Salty Beagle back at the trailer. *That was not fair! I just spent the whole day on a boat in the Cook Inlet fishing, so I must now qualify as a Salty Dog.*

The next day was July 29 and we were back on the boat and headed out to sea. "It's a fine day at sea, Captain!" We saw sea otters, and Captain Ron caught an eel. *Yuck.*

Val loved the sea otters. They had such cute faces and they looked like they would be so much fun to play with. For a second, I thought I'd like to take a swim with them, but then I remembered I hated the water and swimming. I can dog paddle, if need be—but how did the otters swim around on their backs? I was impressed.

The East End Road out of Homer was an experience not to be soon forgotten. It goes out twenty-two miles and takes the traveler so high that our ears were popping. It was paved most of the way, but in places there was no shoulder at all, and the terrain went straight down from the road. We had a great view across Kachemak Bay of three big glaciers, the Grewingk Glacier, the Portlock Glacier, and the Dixon Glacier. We didn't take the road all the way to the end because after leaving the blacktop, the dirt road deteriorated and Dave wanted to be sure we could get back. We were glad we took this awesome ride into the mountains and along the shoreline of Kachemak Bay. As a bonus, we saw a moose crossing the road, and then two moose on a hill having a snack of grass. Dave stopped the truck and made some grunting noises at the moose. They stopped chewing and gave him a good, long stare. I tried to translate Dave's grunts into moose language. I think it was probably something like, "Hey, dummy! Spit out that grass or I'll punch you in the nose."

All too soon, we had to leave our little vacation and the Cook Inlet and return to responsibilities at Denali Park and Preserve. Val said beagles are the best and that I was the salt on her chips.

CHAPTER 8

SAVAGE CABIN AND SAVAGE LOOP TRAIL

"Life is full of beauty. Notice it. Notice the bumble bee, the smallest child, and the smiling faces. Smell the rain, and feel the wind. Live your life to the fullest potential, and fight for your dreams."

Ashley Smith

Just down the road from Savage River Campground is Savage River Cabin. Some of the bus tours stop at the cabin, where an interpretive program is presented. The cabin was built in the 1920s and was still used in the winter as a stop for dogsled teams traveling into the park. There are dog houses scattered around the cabin. The sled dogs stay in them, and their humans stay in the big cabin with heat. *I cannot even fathom this. Although I am not one to shun work, when I'm not working I like warmth and a soft couch, or I like to be tucked between two humans on a big bed. Ok, so I'm spoiled.* This area was only thirteen miles from the main camp at Riley Creek, but 1,000 feet higher in elevation. It was usually cooler by ten degrees than at Riley Creek. The trees were bigger at Riley Creek, and the flowers bloomed about a week earlier than they did at Savage River. It was amazing the difference thirteen miles and 1,000 feet can make in the environment.

Past Savage River Campground was the Savage River Checkpoint and the Loop Trail. To protect the park's resources, the number of vehicles allowed to drive the ninety-mile park road was limited by law.

The checkpoint at the Savage River Bridge ensured that only lawful entries were allowed.

The Loop Trail was a favorite. It started at a parking lot near the entrance to the bridge, followed the river for a mile to a pedestrian bridge, and then a mile back on the other side of the river. Hikers had the option to leave the trail at the pedestrian bridge to climb Mt. Margaret. Whenever we had visitors, we always took them to the Savage Loop Trail. We went there with Kym and Luke, and Lisa and Randy and Grandma Marge. When Natalie and Dan, my human sister and brother-in-law visited we decided to summit Mt. Margaret. After several hours of hiking up Mt. Margaret, we stopped to catch our breath and turned to look back to see how far we had come. We had come a long way, and we could see far from that vantage point. But when we turned around and looked up, we could see there was still a long way from where we stood to the top. We decided that we could claim climbing Mt. Margaret, and that would be almost as good as reaching the summit.

With stealth and precision, you might be able to get close to a Dall sheep, and maybe even get a picture of a huge ram with a full curl. That was our plan as we hiked the mountain. We were told, that in the springtime, if you sit very still, a Dall sheep might even walk right up to you. We continually searched for Dall sheep, but without success. On our way down, we met some nice people from the United Kingdom and stopped to chat. The gentleman said, "Look over on that hill across the river. I think there's a wolf or something." We all strained to see what the man was looking at. "Maybe it's not a wolf, maybe it's a fox," the man said. As we were all still straining to see what he was talking about, the little critter decided to move again, making himself visible among rocks of the same color as his fur. It was not a wolf or a fox. It was a marmot. A marmot is about the size and shape of a woodchuck. It looks nothing like a fox and especially not like a wolf. I guess they don't read *Little Red Riding Hood* in England. If he had, he would have known what a wolf looked like. After that experience he knew what a hoary marmot looked like.

We descended from our perch about halfway up the mountain and proceeded to stroll along the trail by the river. We enjoyed walking along the river and listening to the sounds of the water over rocks and the many different birds providing us with their cheerful melodies. If I had been off leash, I could have done some serious exploring. As it was, I settled for smells along the trail.

One day when we started a hike along the Savage River, we learned there was a baby moose that had been abandoned by its mother. The story was that the mother moose had twins. She crossed the river, but one baby would not follow. The mother left with one twin, and no one had seen her since. A bus driver told us that he had been watching the baby, and its bleats were getting weaker as time went by without any nourishment. When we returned from our hike on the other side of the river to the checkpoint, the baby moose got up and walked down to the river for a drink. There were several photographers lined up with their tripods and cameras, ready to record the baby moose and its fate. If its mother did not return it was doubtful it would live. Since that was not something we wished to witness, we decided it was time to return to camp.

A short distance from the bridge toward Savage Campground, we saw a grizzly bear. If that bear found the baby moose, it would be all over. We know that the park policy was not to interfere with Mother Nature. We wanted no part of seeing a grizzly eat a baby moose, so we went quickly back to camp. The next day we checked with park staff to find out what had happened with the baby moose. There was no evidence of a kill by the river. Maybe his mother had returned and moved him to safer ground. We hoped so.

Baby Moose

CHAPTER 9

FAIRBANKS

"Wilderness to the people of America is a spiritual necessity, an antidote to the high pressure of modern life, a means of regaining serenity and equilibrium."   Sigurd F. Olson

As campground hosts, our schedule was seven days on and seven days off. We took advantage of this schedule to experience as much of Alaska as we could. Fairbanks was the closest big city to the park, and we were able to find hotels willing to let a well-mannered beagle spend the night; so Fairbanks was often where we chose to go on our days off. And before returning to the park, we would stock up with groceries because of the availability of goods and the reduced prices compared to what they charged in Denali Park.

On one of our first trips to Fairbanks, we stopped at Gold Dredge No. 8. Dave and Val learned how a gold dredge worked and had a lesson in panning gold. A gold dredge is a machine that has buckets on the front that scoop up sand, gravel, and dirt that is then sluiced, or washed, over grates that trap the gold. Dredging is one method for getting gold out of the ground, and panning gold involves the fact that gold is a heavy metal that will continually sink to the bottom of a vessel. Dirt with gold in it is placed in a pan with water. The panner swirls the mixture together while washing out the lighter materials. Eventually you get down to black sand and gold. Dave and Val panned and each found some gold, which they combined in a small plastic container. We did not stay long at Gold Dredge No. 8 because we had a reservation for a tour at the Eldorado Gold Mine.

The Eldorado Gold Mine was interesting and fun; more like a Disney production. The tour started out on a train with a singing conductor. The train went down the track a short distance and stopped inside a tunnel. A small area lit up and out stepped a miner, who showed us the layers of sediment before you get to bedrock where the gold was found. The train chugged on and, after leaving the tunnel, it soon came to another small scene with a miner's shack next to a stream. A miner gave a demonstration with a shaker box and gold pan. The third tableau was a steam engine fueled with wood, and a typical mine shaft in the ground.

The last stop seemed like quite a distance from where we had started, and we were finally at the mine. The train and tourists were met by Yukon Yonda and Dexter Clark. Yukon and Dexter escorted us through the rain to an area where the would-be miners lined up along a sluice. Yukon and Dexter described how the sluice worked and then actually made the sluice work right down to panning some gold out of it. From there the tourists were each given a "poke," and taken to an area where they panned for their own gold. Dave and Val were getting pretty good at this by now, and after successfully panning their gold, they were ready to take it inside the cook shack and have it weighed. They added their gold from the dredge and ended up with $54 in gold.

While Dave and Val were waiting for the train to take them back to the starting point, Dave was snooping around. He discovered that the mine was directly behind the starting point. The train just took us on a ride and gave us the impression that we were traveling far away from the station to the mine. In spite of this knowledge, Dave and Val waited for the train and didn't give the secret away to anyone.

Gold Dredge No. 8

After hitting the mother lode, Dave and Val headed for Chena Hot Springs, where there was a small rustic campground; a hotel that did not accommodate dogs; a restaurant; a gift shop; an ice house; sled dogs; hiking trails; and, of course hot springs. Dave and Val loved the hot springs, which was an anomaly to me. They returned there as often as they could arrange it. Whatever ... let them have their fun. I enjoyed walking in the woods; sniffing along the creek; and, my favorite, was getting the sled dogs fired up. What a cacophony!

Tableau from Eldorado Gold Mine Train

77

Even though we really liked Chena Hot Springs, we had to be up and out early because our next adventure awaited in Fairbanks.

Chena Hot Springs

Lisa and Marge

There was a line of people waiting to board the riverboat. Val noticed a lot of debris coming down the river, like whole trees with root systems. She mentioned to Dave that she wondered if it was safe to be taking this boat trip due to the fact that the river was flooding and there was a large amount of material floating in the water. The lady standing behind us in line said that she asked about the safety of traveling down the river in flood stage, and the man at the counter said it was perfectly safe. Val said, "Yeah, well that's what they told people on the *Titanic*!" In spite of Val's fears, we got on the riverboat and took our chances. Unlike the people on the *Titanic*, we didn't have far to swim to the shore.

Riverboat Discovery Day!

The river was higher than it had been since the 1967 floods, so we saw the river in a much different way than most tourists. The trip began with a float plane demonstration. Mr. Lewis, our trip narrator, was talking to the pilot and we could hear both sides of the conversation over the loud speakers on the boat. The float plane took off and landed on the river in full view of us. I remembered what our friend Ron Palm told us when we asked him why he didn't have a plane. He said he doesn't fly because too many of his friends who flew small planes were no longer with us. *Yikes!* I have big beagle ears, and when I stick my head out of the truck window while Dave is driving, I sometimes feel as though I could fly.

There were some interesting sights on our trip upriver. We saw flooded properties, and we stopped at Susan Butcher's dog kennels.

Susan Butcher and her team won the Iditarod dogsled race four times. She was the first woman to ever win the race. Unfortunately, she died of cancer some years ago, but her family still ran the kennel. Mr. Lewis told us that after Susan Butcher won the race a few times, t-shirts were available that said, "Alaska, where men are men, and women win the Iditarod!" Mr. Lewis talked to a musher on the shore, and she explained how they trained the sled dogs. I wished I could get off the boat and train with the sled dogs for a week or two. It would be like doggy boot camp. I would be a lean, mean fighting machine after that. Just look at the muscles on those sled dogs. Close your eyes and imagine me leading a pack of dogs out into the wild. How awesome would that be?! The only thing I wouldn't like about it was that the sleds worked better on snow, and I prefer warm and dry—like on the couch.

Butcher Kennels

The next stop on the riverboat cruise was at a reproduction of an Athabasca Indian village called Chena Village. As the boat pulled up to the village, someone cued the reindeer and they came out to greet the ship. When the boat was tied up, an Athabasca woman named Dixie Anderson got on the boat to present a fashion show of Athabasca clothing. She designed and manufactured beautiful parkas, dresses, and other items of clothing. Dixie made a parka that is on display at the Smithsonian in Washington, D.C. As far as I was concerned, she knew how to make a coat. What wonderful out-of-this-world smells. Fantastic! I just want to snuggle up in one.

We also learned that "Athabasca Indians traditionally lived along the major river ways of interior Alaska. The Athabascas lived as far south as the Kenai Peninsula and as far north as the Brooks Range. Before any contact with the "outside," they were nomadic. Today many still live a subsistence lifestyle that includes summer fish camps. They are very attached to family groups in which sharing and respecting every living thing is important. Traditionally, men lived with their wife's family for the first year of marriage and children were part of the mother's clan. Athabasca tradition called for elders to make all major decisions. Caribou and moose hide were the main components of clothing, and Athabascas used canoes made out of birch bark, moose hide, and cottonwood for summer transportation (Your Guide to the Chena Village, compliments of the Riverboat Discovery)."

Walking through the village, we saw many interesting things, such as the Post Office with a grass roof, a garden with cabbages the size of a washing machines, a fishing wheel, and indigenous housing.

Chena Village Post Office

Dixie Anderson showed us how to fillet a salmon without removing the tail, so it could be hung to dry. The Athabascas dried a lot of fish; keeping the better salmon for their own consumption and the less desirable ones they fed to the dogs. Dried fish was perfect for dog sledding because it was lightweight and full of protein. I was ready to try it out, but no luck. I wondered if it was as good as halibut.

This is what 23 hours of sunlight per day will produce!

Athabasca Fishing Wheel

We always had a blast in Fairbanks. During one of our visits, Dave thought it would be great fun to drive to the Arctic Circle, which was only about two hundred miles from Fairbanks. Just being able to say that we had traveled inside the Arctic Circle would be cool. As we headed north out of Fairbanks, we stopped at the Alyeska Pipeline. We were able to get directions to just about anywhere …

Things called "pigs" are in the pipe to smooth the flow of oil and make it easier to pump. *Gosh, the things you learn on a trip.* We did not know why they called these things pigs. It didn't look like a pig, and it sure didn't smell like one. We decided to leave the pig there and contemplate what other kinds of animals we might see on our way to the Arctic Circle.

There is more than oil inside the pipe

The road we were on was the same road that the ice-road truckers take on their way to Prudhoe. I settled down in the backseat because it was obvious that this trip would take a while. Before I knew it, Dave was slamming on the brakes and jumping out of the truck. The truck door was left open so I jumped out of the truck right behind him. The sight in front of us was frightening and got the adrenaline pumping. There—in the middle of the road—was a huge grizzly bear circling a mother moose and her calf. Dave stayed back from the scene to snap pictures. The mother moose lunged at the grizzly with her head down, but I knew that

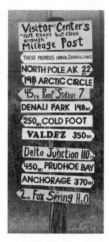

any minute that grizzly bear would get the baby moose. I just couldn't stand it, so I started howling my best beagle howl—and the bear turned to look at me. He paused for a moment and then evidently decided that I would make an easier meal than the baby moose and headed in my direction. *Yikes! Grizzly bears are big and fast.* I scooted back to the truck as fast as I could. Dave was still not in the truck, so I did some fancy moves around the truck to avoid the bear while Dave got in. After I avoided some close calls when the bear reached under the truck to get me, I jumped in the truck and Dave hit the gas. Luckily the distraction provided an opportunity for the moose and her baby to escape. *Thank goodness! Remington Beagle what a hero you are.*

"Remington. Remington. Wake up! We're getting out to walk around the town of Livengood. You were having a pretty good dream there, buddy. Your legs were really moving, like you were running a race." *I was running a race—from a bear. I guess I am only a hero in my dreams.*

The sign said: Livengood. No services. And they mean no services. There was a weather station, some highway equipment, and a couple unoccupied rustic cabins. That was Livengood. There was not a person in sight. When we listened to the weather station back at Savage Camp, we heard the weather report from Livengood every day. The picture in our minds for Livengood was quite different from the reality.

Our vision of driving to the Arctic Circle was different from the reality as well. The road was very curvy and there was a lot of patchy fog that day. We took a vote on whether or not a white-knuckle drive for another 100 miles was worth it. Three to zip, we decided to return to Fairbanks.

As we neared Fairbanks, we saw a beautiful river and decided to try our luck at some fishing, and maybe finding some gold. We also discovered a town that was smaller than Livengood: Olnes, population of one.

Because we ended our drive to the Arctic Circle, we had some extra time to spend in Fairbanks. We decided to visit the University of Alaska, Fairbanks Large Animal Research Station, where they raise musk ox. The musk ox, also called muskox and musk-ox, were not as big as Dave thought they would be, but interesting nonetheless. Musk ox were native to Alaska but were hunted to extinction. Since being reintroduced to the state many years ago, they have flourished in the wild on the northwest coast of Alaska. Their coat is harvested and makes a fabulous yarn.

The museum at the University of Alaska, Fairbanks was really something. The experience started on the outside as the building itself was fabulous. The sweeping roofline was reminiscent of the Opera House in Sydney, Australia. The museum houses amazing exhibits, such as Blue Babe, a 36,000-year-old bison. Take a whiff of that! (I couldn't because it was inside a glass case.) The Alaskan art collection was extensive. They had everything from ancient ivory carvings to modern photographs from the collection of Michio Hoshino. Mr. Hoshino photographed much of Alaska and its wildlife. His work is well known in Alaska, and much loved by all. As a beagle connoisseur of fine art, I appreciated all of these displays, especially the bison. I don't want to question Dave's intellect, but I he seemed to favor the outhouse exhibit.

One of our favorite places in Fairbanks was Pioneer Park. It consisted of a village of vintage houses, cabins, a hotel, and a theatre. The buildings had all been moved to Pioneer Park from their original locations and arranged in a village setting. They were filled with museums, restaurants, and shops. Most of the shops sold items made in Alaska. There was a fun, little train that skirted the whole park, a riverboat to explore, and a train car used by President Harding on his trip to Alaska.

When in Fairbanks, we always took the opportunity to eat at the Salmon Bake, a restaurant in Pioneer Park that offered both inside and outside eating areas. The entrance to the restaurant was like going through a mine shaft. It opened into a park area with picnic tables. After paying for your meal, you were awarded a fish-shaped plate that you could fill up at their extensive buffet. There was a sign at one station giving the diner a choice between a hot dog or crab legs. Lisa said that our sister Natalie would have to give that choice some serious consideration. It's true. Nothing like a good hot dog. Having said that, I will just say that the prime rib was exquisite, and the halibut was also outstanding.

My human sister Lisa, her husband, Randy, and my human grandmother Marge loved the ambiance and the great food at the Salmon Bake. On one of our visits there, Lisa actually climbed on the carved wooden statue of the salmon out front and had her picture taken. There was absolutely no limit to what these humans would do. Val said that I am the butter on her dinner roll.

My favorite part of Fairbanks was visiting Creamer's Field, a large waterfowl refuge. There were lots of sandhill cranes and Canada geese and a multitude of other birds. I was allowed to go on the trails with Dave and Val as long as I was on a leash. It was great. There were some wonderful smells there!

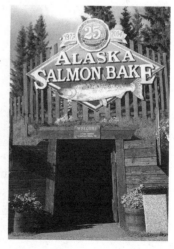

This refuge actually started out as a dairy farm. The Creamers (great name for dairy farm owners) had a dairy farm in Fairbanks for many years. When the farm was no longer operational it still attracted many migrating birds. A group called Friends of Creamer's Field raised money to make the farm a refuge and to maintain it. There are several trails and places to view the birds. Val said I am cooler than a Canada Goose!

It was time to head back to Denali Park and our job. As we left Fairbanks, the large and deep Tanana Valley was as pretty as we had ever seen it. The sky was a beautiful azure and the clouds were white and puffy. The highway ran along a top ridge of the mountain, giving us a bird's-eye view of the valley. The rocky tops of mountains were blurred by distance and formed a purple contrast to the white and blue sky. The purple softened to a light-green above the tree line, and then the color darkened to the dark-green and black of the spruce that clung to the side of the mountain as they joined the aspen and scrub birch nearer the bottom. The valley floor displayed some ponds and lakes that add blues to contrast the green.

Standing on the ridgetop and looking out over the valley we could feel the fresh breeze on our faces, smell the pine-scented forest, and appreciate the immenseness. This valley takes your breath away with its size and beauty, and at the same time you realize its (and your own) insignificance in the universe. We never tired of this drive; around every bend there was a new surprise.

The splendor of the Tanana Valley is juxtaposed against a tableau of Alaskan imagination. Tucked into a hill was a sofa covered with large stuffed animals and other toys. It begs the question: Why?

Finally, we were on the park road and almost at camp. We saw that there was something happening up ahead. It was a moose jam. A moose jam is unlike any other jam you may know. It's not like strawberry jam or grape jam. It's not even a bunch of moose all jammed together. It was a traffic jam caused by stopped buses and private vehicles so that people could take pictures of the moose near the road. Sometimes you think it's a moose jam and it's really a bear jam. Neither one of them is good on toast.

CHAPTER 10

NENANA

*"The wilderness holds answers to more questions than we have
yet learned to ask."*   *Nancy Wynne Newhall*

Nenana, between Fairbanks and the park, was always a pleasant place
to stop and break up our trip. This is where the Nenana and the Tanana
rivers meet, which makes it prone to floods. In recorded history,
significantly in 1967 and recently in 2008, there were major floods at
this confluence of rivers. We witnessed the 2008 flood on one of our
trips to and from Fairbanks for supplies.

Nenana was also Jack Coghill's hometown. He has served as
mayor, legislator, lieutenant governor, and was a writer of the Alaska
Constitution.

We enjoyed the museum in the railroad depot at Nenana. The
railroad was completed through Nenana in 1923. President Warren
Harding came to Alaska and drove the golden spike to finish the project
at the north end of the railroad bridge that connected the railroad
coming south from Fairbanks to the track coming from Anchorage
north to Nenana. He traveled in a special railroad car that can still be
viewed at Pioneer Park in Fairbanks. The railroad continues to be a
critical link between Fairbanks and Anchorage. A road link, the George
Parks Highway, wasn't completed until 1971.

At the railroad depot, we saw ledgers of past Ice Classic records,
going back to the early 1900s. The ledgers listed all of the bets placed

as to when ice break up would occur each spring on the Tanana River. A large tripod was placed on the frozen river and connected to a clock. People placed bets on the exact minute when the ice would break up. This annual event was important because that meant the river would then soon be open to traffic. Supplies could come in and people would have the ability to travel by boat. When the ice weakened to the point that the tripod moved and stopped the clock, the winner was determined. Gamblers from all over Alaska placed bets and many millions have been paid out in prize money. Alaskans have such ingenuity! They took ice melting and turned it into a fun, money-making lottery! Bravo!

Have you heard of Balto, the sled dog that led a team safely across the ice to Nome with antitoxin to save the people of Nome from a diphtheria epidemic? In 1925, the Alaska Railroad brought a supply of diphtheria antitoxin from Anchorage to Nenana, and then a dog sled team left from Nenana, carrying the antitoxin to Nome. The Iditarod Race was inspired by this heroic run, although it now starts from various locations, most recently from Willow, Alaska.

Balto was to me what Superman is to humans. In my dreams, I am Balto—leading my team through hazardous weather and across dangerous ice to save the day. In reality, I am more like a couch potato—but a guy can dream, can't he?

Val liked Nenana for its gift shops and the Native Cultural Center. I liked the time out of the truck to walk along the river's edge, sniff all kinds of new exciting smells, and dream about being a hero sled dog.

CHAPTER 11

THE TRESTLE

"We do not inherit the earth from our ancestors; we borrow it from our children."　　　　　　　　　　*Native American*

It was a joyous day in the park when the trestle for the railroad going from Anchorage to Fairbanks, Alaska, was completed across Riley Creek. The first superintendent of the park made a plan for his headquarters to be near where the train would cross Riley Creek because he projected that it would be where future visitors would enter the park. His first choice for the site was not available because Maurice Morino owned the land and was building a large roadhouse in anticipation of the railroad station that was to be located just north of Riley Creek. Eventually, Morino owned and operated a roadhouse and cabins at McKinley Station. The community that formed near the railroad station included park employees, roadhouse operators, and trappers and hunters.

At the base of the trestle that crossed Riley Creek was a place known as "the hole." This was where people made and sold moonshine, and prostitutes hung out. The McKinley Station children were forbidden to go near there because their parents did not want them subjected to the bad language and behavior that was exhibited there. When Val learned of this not widely known history, she had to go check it out. Gentlemen that we are, Dave and I could not possibly let her go alone. We drove to the current train station, parked the truck, and hiked along the tracks in the direction of Riley Creek. When we got to the railroad trestle, we looked for a place to walk down to the creek. Although it looked pretty steep, we took a chance and headed down, grasping on bushes to avoid a painful slide to the bottom.

Once at the bottom, we found a trail that led both ways along the creek. We obviously chose the most difficult way to the base of the trestle because there were trails leading to it. Humans pride themselves on their abilities to think and resolve problems. Not so much these two. A quick stop at the visitor's center would have given Dave and Val the information they needed to walk safely to the base of the trestle—but no, we had to slide down a nearly perpendicular slope, getting scratched and bruised. Had I been alone, I never would have chosen that path, but where my humans go I go. Fortunately, none of us were injured.

We chose to walk on the trail toward where Riley Creek empties into the Nenana River, looking along both sides of the trail for signs of an old community. We found some old stone foundations; an old, rusted-out pail; and evidence of water storage. We found the hole! We wondered about the hard-scrabble life the people who lived down the hill and by the creek. It surely was not an easy one, especially in the winter. Wood had to be cut and water had to be carried. Food had to be hunted or gathered. The folks who lived in the hole worked hard just to stay alive; much like the people up on the hill who believed that they were better than the trash living down by the creek.

We walked back past the base of the trestle and headed the other way along the trail. Wow! All kinds of trails, one even went over a small wooden walking bridge across the creek. As we continued along the trail, Val spied what she thought was a tent by the creek. Dave thought it was a tent as well. It's probably someone camping illegally!

Down through the brush we went, with branches and sticks scratching on contact. Finally, we arrived near the tent site to find that it was a very big tent-shaped rock. Nothing to report to headquarters.

Moving on, we took a trail up the hill and found the site where Maurice Morino had his roadhouse. Unfortunately, it burned down in the 1950s so there was nothing to see except a sign commemorating the site. Casually strolling past the Morino roadhouse site, we soon came to the train station and our truck. It started to rain pretty hard when we still had the equivalent of a couple city blocks to walk, so we all got wet. Back in the cab of the truck, I suddenly realized how unpleasant the smell of wet humans really is. It's nasty.

After soothing our wounds at camp and the rain stopping, Val and I decided to go for a walk. As we turned the corner by campsite number twenty-four, a red squirrel darted in front of me and then up a big black spruce tree. Red squirrels get their thrills by tormenting me. The other day, two of them were cursing and chasing each other. They were so intent on the chase, they didn't realize they were headed directly at me. I stopped to see how close they would get before they realized they were heading into the jaws of a ferocious dog. They got within two feet of me before they suddenly put on the brakes, left skid marks in the dirt of the road, and did perfect backflips before heading off in two directions. Safely ensconced in the trees, they cursed me in "red squirrel." Beagles are not fluent in that language, but I knew enough to know when I was being cursed. Someone should teach those bad boys some manners. Val said, "Sticks and stones, Remington. Sticks and stones." So I just ignored them and continued on our walk.

Talking about confrontations with park animals, early one morning as I was doing rounds with Val we walked straight into a cow moose. I'm guessing we were about twelve to fifteen feet away from it. We were scared because we had learned in our training that moose look at all dogs as if they are wolves, and wolves are their natural enemy. Their instinct is to trample us to death. I was so scared that I could not make a sound, which turned out to be a good thing because the moose, which from my perspective was as big as a bus, decided I was not a threat. She turned away from us and charged into the forest. My reward for not bellowing was a good sniff of the road where the moose had walked – for me almost as good as a sniff of the real thing. Val said that I am her hero – she loves me as much as ice cream on her apple pie.

CHAPTER 12

FLYING FIXED-WING

"It's only when you're flying above it that you realize how incredible the Earth really is."　　　　*Philippe Perrin*

Ruth Glacier flows from Mt. Denali. As our fixed-wing airplane descended to land on the glacier, I thought for sure we were going to crash into the mountainside. But the pilot was a retired Navy pilot and he sat us down on the glacier perfectly; then taxied around to leave the plane in position to take off again. I thought about the numerous times this pilot had performed this landing and wondered if he did this landing with some kind of perverse pleasure, knowing that his passengers were holding their breath and saying prayers. We deplaned and had to put our sunglasses on right away because the reflection from sunshine on the snow of the glacier was blinding. Denali was closer than we had ever seen it—beautiful and forbidding. The pilot explained there were thousands of feet of ice beneath our feet plus many feet of snow on top of the ice.

From our landing spot on Ruth Glacier, we could see the house and outhouse that Don Sheldon had built. Don Sheldon was an air-taxi driver out of Talkeetna, Alaska. He was well known in the interior for his flying prowess. So, when homesteads were offered, he decided to homestead on Ruth Glacier. He built a house and an outhouse on a rocky outcropping adjacent to Ruth Glacier with Denali in the background. Some years later, the government decided it hadn't really meant that someone could homestead on a glacier, and they tried to get the property back. They took the Sheldon family to court but, in this case, the government lost and the Sheldon family still owned their property on the glacier. They rent out the cabin by the week, and it is booked way into the future. Renters fly in with all of the gear and food they will need for a week and then fly out with everything—including their waste material (the outhouse is off limits). The pilot said that he flew a couple to the glacier to get married, and then they spent their honeymoon in the cabin. I wouldn't mind staying there, but once you have sniffed one pile of snow you have pretty much sniffed them all.

There were other small planes on the glacier with us. We watched as one of them took off. It taxied down the glacier and then dropped out of sight. It was alarming to witness the disappearance of the plane, but eventually we could see it again. By the time it came into view, it was miles away and appeared to be the size of a toy.

The half hour on the glacier was soon over, and the nine-passenger plane was loaded for the return trip to Healy. Seats were assigned by weight on these little planes. Val was near the front and Dave was in the back of the plane. Let's not talk about where they put dogs. Dave had an anxious moment on the way back when the girl sitting next to him asked for a "Healy Parachute," which is actually a barf bag. Fortunately, she did not have to use it. As our plane flew through the Alaska Range, back toward Healy, it appeared that we were coming very close to the sheer rock sides of the mountains, but we were actually a quarter mile or more away. (Or so the pilot said.) This was an experience that we highly recommend. Wow!

Another flight opportunity out of Healy, Alaska, was a Mt. Denali summit flight. The day we took that flight was beautiful and cloudless. There was so much to see from the air. The aerial view of the park road was stupendous, and we even saw Savage River Campground and our trailer. We can affirm that the Polychrome Mountains are aptly named, and the Muldoon Glacier was in stark contrast with the surrounding mountains.

It gets very cold above 10,000 feet, and we had little oxygen masks so we wouldn't get goofy. The plane flew around Denali one way and then back the other way so that people on both sides of the plane could take pictures. Looking at the mountain close-up was ethereal. At 20,310 feet, Mt. Denali is the highest mountain on the North American continent. It has been pushed up by tectonic pressure by the Pacific Plate, the same culprit that caused many earthquakes in Alaska.

The native Koyukon Athabascans called the mountain Denali. A gold prospector called the mountain McKinley in support of presidential candidate William McKinley from Ohio, and that name was the official name from 1917 to 2015, when it was changed to Denali. Although our pilot told us that our plane was miles away from the mountain, it appeared to us that we could hit the summit with a snowball from the outside of the plane. We knew we would never look at this mountain the same again. I'm sure those who have summited the mountain, or even attempted a summit, never look at it the same either.

The first to summit the north peak (the highest peak) was the team led by Hudson Stuck and Harry Karstens on June 7, 1913. Harry Karstens later became the first superintendent of McKinley National Park (now known as Denali National Park and Preserve). Many have attempted to summit the mountain since that time, and many have died. While we were working at Savage Camp it was announced that the search for some Japanese climbers was ending without success. That information quickly turns your perspective of the mountain from majestic and elegant to cold and cruel. May they rest in peace.

Denali

We were grateful when we landed without incident at the Healy Airport, mostly because our pilot appeared to be a teenager. We asked the driver that took us back to Denali Park if the pilot was old enough to have a driver's license, which caused our driver to laugh. We probably should have kept our thoughts to ourselves and avoided teasing the pilot. Youthful as he was, he did a very good job and brought us back safely. What a great time we had that day!

CHAPTER 13

RIDING THE SHUTTLE BUS

"If you can't be in awe of Mother Nature, there's something wrong with you."
Alex Trebek

Over one hundred thousand people visit the park each year to experience the beauty and the wildlife. At the same time, the wildlife needs its environment protected. The problem becomes how to get 100,000 plus people into the park without disrupting the ecosystem. The answer was buses. Tourists can choose between a narrated bus tour into the park or a shuttle bus. If you want to get off of the shuttle and hike around, that is permissible, and when you are ready to ride again just flag down the next shuttle.

There are various tours into the park; the buses go from the entrance as far as Kantishna, at mile 92 of the park road. We packed a lunch and chose the shuttle to Eielson Visitor Center at mile 66. We stopped at Teklanika River and got off the bus. There was a lookout deck and we learned about braided rivers. Water always travels where the resistance is the least. These rivers are fed from glaciers in the mountains. Glacial silt settles to the bottom and eventually clogs up one spot and so the river heads off in another direction. Consecutive seasons find the appearance of these rivers very different.

Denali from the park road

This road offers spots along the way that provide breathtaking views of Denali. Denali is so big it creates its own weather system. Depending on the distance, angle, availability of light, and whether or not there are clouds shrouding the mountain, Denali will look different on an hourly and daily basis. The mountain does not often stand stark-white against a bright-blue sky. More often there are clouds covering all or part of the view. Sometimes you have to look twice because it appears to be just a watermark in the sky.

Visitors to the park want to basically see two things: the mountain and the wildlife. Most trips along the park road offer some kind of wildlife viewing. As the bus travels the park road, riders are told to shout if they see wildlife and the driver will stop. On this trip, we saw a grizzly bear by the side of the road, a large male moose, some caribou in a far-off valley, a very large beaver in a pond, a golden eagle, a Dall sheep, and some ground squirrels.

Eielson was named after Carl Eielson, who learned how to fly during World War I. While attending college in Washington, D.C., he met the representative from the then territory of Alaska, who enticed him to go to Alaska. He returned to flying there and flew the first airmail route. Eielson did flight exploring, landing the plane on drift ice, and flying over the North Pole to Europe. He established Alaskan Airlines. He was killed in a crash in Siberia.

The visitor's center named for him is built into the mountain. The area provides amazing views of Denali as well as wonderful hiking opportunities. As the bus slowed down to pull into the parking lot at Eielson, we saw a beautiful fox at the edge of the road. The fox had something in its mouth. We're not sure what that something was because the fox hurried into the brush.

There were picnic tables outside at the Eielson Visitor Center, and as we ate our lunch, we were entertained by a ground squirrel. We think someone may have broken the rules against feeding wildlife because this ground squirrel was obviously looking for a handout.

We decided to extend our trip beyond Eielson and got on a shuttle to Wonder Lake, which was at mile 85 of the park road. We saw a pair of swans on Wonder Lake and walked through the campground. There was a tent-only campground with potable water and restrooms, and a seasonal campground host. Although this spot was known for its mosquito infestations, we were not bothered. One of the reasons we wanted to travel this far out into the park was for a closer view of Denali, but alas, the majestic mountain was shrouded in clouds.

Kantishna was the end of the park road. Once a gold-mining mecca, much of this area was now privately owned, but visitors can stop at the Fannie Quigley house for some history of the area. Fannie was the quintessential Alaskan who lived out her days in the harsh wilderness. There were currently a few privately-owned businesses and an airstrip. On the way back to camp Val said I am the caramel in her candy bar.

Park Road

CHAPTER 14

A TRIP TO BARROW

"Love is our true destiny. We do not find the meaning of life by ourselves alone—we find it with another." Thomas Merton

Why did we choose to go to Barrow, the northernmost community on the North American continent? Bragging rights, curiosity, historical significance, or just because it was there? Our small group of four humans—Natalie, Dan, Dave, and Val—and one counselor dog, Remington, were excited to begin the adventure. The flight left Fairbanks and flew over the Brooks Range for the first stop at Prudhoe Bay. Beyond the Brooks Range of mountains, all the way to the Arctic Ocean, are miles and miles of dirt and rock with an occasional kettle pond. There was a brief touchdown at Prudhoe before we continued the flight to Barrow.

Russell, from our tour company, greeted us at the airport in Barrow. Russell was an Inupiat Eskimo who loved Barrow and was happy to share it with us. The first stop was the Will Rogers, Wiley Post monument. These two men crashed their airplane near Barrow in 1935. They were both famous people for their time. Wiley Post was searching for a better route to Siberia through Alaska. He was a famous pilot and invented the first space suit. Will Rogers was a famous newspaper columnist and comedian. I have to say that Will Rogers was my favorite because he said, "If there are no dogs in heaven, then when

I die I want to go where they went." All dogs do go to heaven, Will Rogers. Everyone knows that.

Our next stop was the ancient village of Ukpiagvik. It did not look like a village, it looked like mounds of dirt. The ancient Eskimos built their houses by digging into the earth. They used whale ribs and driftwood with animal skins stretched over them and added sod on top of that for their houses. There was usually a firepit in the center of the structure with an opening above it. Around the edge of the interior room, they would build a ledge. The ledges were used to sleep on. They dug notches in which to store food and other things. We were actually able to see one of these ancient houses, where the sea had washed away the dirt covering of the structure. There was a photo opportunity nearby where you could put your face in a hole to make you look like a native. *Cute, but no thanks.*

Even though Barrow was a small community, the choices for lunch were varied. We could choose from Mexican food, Chinese food, or pizza. We chose Pepe's. Pepe's was presented as a Mexican restaurant, but it was really quite eclectic. We ordered cheeseburgers and fries. While we waited for our food, we soaked in some of the atmosphere. There was a stuffed space alien on the end of the salad bar, the side door was propped open with a shovel, and the long-stemmed yellow roses on the counter were beautiful—about a week ago. I supposed that when you received roses in Barrow, you held onto them as long as possible. They had to have been flown in from somewhere. It was reported that the ladies room was clean, but if you were looking for privacy, you may have had trouble shutting the stall door. There was a hinge at the top inside of the door, but the bottom hinge was on the outside. I'm sure that has been fixed by now. All in all, we loved Pepe's. It was a fun atmosphere, the food was good, and the price was fair.

After lunch, Russell transported the tour group to the cultural center. We were entertained by some native Barrowians who danced to music provided by drummers. Next was the blanket toss, a traditional game. The blanket was made from seal and walrus skins, and could also be used as a covering for their whaling boats called *umiaks*. They had sewn handles all around the edge of the blanket. A local young person, who had volunteered to be tossed, climbed onto the raised blanket. The participants doing the tossing were instructed to pull on their handles, and then release the handle inward just a little. They pulled on the handle again, inward and outward, causing the blanket to flex up and down and making it like a trampoline. A combination of the moving blanket and the person on the blanket jumping, caused the person to go higher and higher into the air. We were told that the jumper can go as high as thirty feet in the air. This almost never happens when *chechakos* (people from the outside) are working the blanket.

We loved watching the young people taking part in demonstrations of their ancient culture. I connected this culture sharing to times when my inner-wolf comes out. My inner-wolf does not demonstrate bravery, hunting skills, or cunning. My inner-wolf comes through in the manipulation for a treat; undying loyalty; and, of course, great intelligence.

We were able to spend some time walking around Barrow on our own. We checked out the local police station, a convenience store, and the hotel. One of our stops was at a grocery store. Everything was more expensive than we were used to paying, especially items like fresh produce and dairy products. We learned that some of the local population worked for the government, some worked for the tribe, some worked at the college, some worked for the oil companies, and some were unemployed and on assistance.

When we commenced our tour with Russell on the bus, we saw the local college and the high school football field. The field was covered with Astroturf and the bleachers on the far side were really close to the ocean. We drove out on a peninsula of land and saw palm trees made with whale baleen, seal meat drying, and the carcass of a beached whale. We were able to put our feet (and paws) in both the Beaufort and Chukchi Seas of the Arctic Ocean. To round out our experience, we stopped at an arch made of whale ribs. Classic.

We had time to pause and contemplate our Barrow visit while we waited for our flight back to Fairbanks. Pampered city dwellers that we are, we wondered why people would choose to live where the weather conditions were so harsh and where for many months, they lived in total darkness.

Russell gave us some insight. He told us that he went to college "outside," but returned to his hometown after getting his degree. He showed us where his grandma lived, and we waved to his uncle and cousin who were on a four-wheeler ordering coffee from a drive-thru. They were a hearty bunch; ingenious in their inventions and survival tactics. They stayed because Barrow was their home. It was who they are and what and who they love.

CHAPTER 15

FUN THINGS IN AND NEAR THE PARK

*"Keep close to Nature's heart ... and break clear away once in
a while, and climb a mountain or spend a week in the woods.
Wash your spirit clean."*   John Muir

The next big adventure for the group was a rafting trip down the
Nenana River. The outfitter dressed the rafters in wet suits, complete
with gloves and hats. This fun-filled trip started from the McKinley
Chalet in Glitter Gulch and went to the bridge next to the power plant
in Healy. Our guide, Lisa, was as cute as a button. She was an equal
opportunity raft guide and gave "glacial facials" to everyone on the raft.

It was a good thing they suited you up from head to toe, because
the water comes at you from all directions, and it was cold. Lisa told
us that the river was mostly category 2 and 3 rapids right now because
the water was low. When the water was high, the rapids were primarily
category 3 and 4. She pointed out some spots that were classified as 5's,
but we avoided going through those. The perspective from the river
through the canyon while clutching the handle on the raft was not only
precarious and exciting, but beautiful as well.

We had driven over the bridge spanning the Nenana River in the
canyon and had seen the rafters, but being there was the best. Even
though it was August and the air was warm, we were very cold by the
time we reached Healy by river. We were happy to board a school bus

and get warm while the workers loaded the rafts for trailering back to the gulch.

Since rafting the Nenana was not enough excitement for one day, we decided to climb Mt. Healy. There was a trail that led the way. Up and up we went; pausing along the way to catch our breath. The higher we went, the more dynamic the views. We watched the train pull out of McKinley Station and visually followed it along the winding tracks like a snake with a bright-yellow and blue head. About halfway up the mountain, we met a group of people coming down who had an encounter with a grizzly bear. Two young women from this group had hiked ahead when they came upon a bear. They did the worst thing possible, they ran away from the bear. The bear chased them, but they were able to catch up with the larger group before the bear caught up with them. The bigger group of people evidently discouraged the bear from continuing the chase, and it did not molest the group. The girls were sufficiently shaken up, so their group was heading down the mountain as quickly as they could.

Being fearless, our group continued up the mountain. When we got about three-quarters of the way up the mountain, we met up with another group of people heading down. This group had also seen the bear. They were part of a larger group that had reached the top of the ridge. They had descended to a position on the mountain below the bear when it emerged on the trail. So the bear was between them and the rest of their group on top of the mountain. The hikers at the top could not descend due to the bear hanging out on the trail, sizing up which of the hikers looked like a good lunch. Needless to say, the hikers at the top were staying put. The hikers below the bear decided that if they came down the mountain they would give the bear room to wander away, and the group at the top could then come down. All of this information gave our little group enough information to concede the mountain to the bear and descend. We never did hear if those people at the top got down ... maybe they are still up there.

Just after supper that night, Dave tapped on the window and pointed out a coyote in the road right in front of our trailer. Val rushed outside to get a picture. When I barked, the coyote turned and stared at me. He was trying to intimidate me, but I was not the least bit scared. My ace in the hole was Dave. He would never let that coyote get me. We had seen wolves in and around the camp, but this was the first coyote.

My human sister, Natalie, found a sizeable hunk of fur lying on a bush down by Jenny Creek. It was definitely not fur from a snowshoe hare. It looked like wolf or coyote fur. Natalie was pretty sure she saw a wolf in a walk down by the creek, and when my human sister Kym was here, she took a photo of a large wolf print by the creek in the same area. So the fur could have been wolf or coyote. Maybe a wolf attacked a coyote. Or maybe it was an intrepid beagle who grabbed a wolf by the throat, and with powerful beagle jaws tore a huge chunk out of that wolf's throat as a warning not to do anything nefarious. Then the fearless beagle left the fur there as a warning to other wolves not to enter his territory. *Yeah. That's what happened.*

CHAPTER 16

FLOWERS, BIRDS, AND BEARS

"I can find God in nature, in animals, in birds, and in the environment."   Pat Buckley

There are many varieties of wildflowers in the park. I loved the bluebells, and they were Val's favorite too. I should clarify that although bluebells are my favorite flower, they are not my favorite smell. My favorite smell would be something like a rotting Snowshoe hare carcass.

The lupine are among the first plants to flower in the park; we saw lupine blossoms in June at Savage Campground. Lupine are from the pea family, but our book on flowers told us that they were "probably poisonous if eaten." After the beautiful blooms left, much too soon, we noticed the seed pods and we agreed that the seed pods did look like peapods. We were glad we had a resource that told us lupine was a plant that should not be eaten, otherwise we might have tried cooking the seeds with some butter or maybe a cream sauce. The lupine in Savage Campground were lovely, but as we traveled around Alaska, we found bigger ones in huge, lush patches at lower elevations.

As the lupine faded, the fireweed was just coming on. The state flower of Alaska was the Forget-Me-Not. We traveled from Barrow to Homer in Alaska without seeing any Forget-Me-Nots. Fireweed, on the other hand, was prolific. Well, not in Barrow, but pretty much everywhere else around the state. Our opinion was that if fireweed couldn't be the state flower maybe it could be the state weed.

The fireweed was so pretty, and huge patches grew along the roadside and sides of the mountains. In the springtime, you might wonder why this plant was called fireweed. Both varieties of fireweed have beautiful pink blossoms that look nothing like fire. However, when the colors turn in the fall, the leaves of the plant turn bright-red, and those leaves pointed upward in abundance from the stem look very much like tongues of fire. When the plants go to seed, a fine fluffy substance with seeds attached is carried by the wind, producing abundant fireweed for future generations.

Val had a recipe for fireweed jelly. We had to go outside the park and collect fireweed blossoms to make a tea, and then jelly from the tea. It was pretty good, but questionable if it was worth the work. We needed something like 200 blossoms. You can also make fireweed honey. We didn't have any bee hives so we didn't try the honey. Also, in the spring, the shoots are edible, but we didn't try that either.

Monkshood was also a favorite flower of Val's. It did resemble a monk's hood. The terrain where it grew was very rugged in spots, and some places it looked as if the plants were growing through the rock. And the foxtails coming up out of the hard ground were an anomaly to Val, who couldn't grow flowers with potting soil and fertilizer.

Eskimo potato, a mainstay of the grizzly bear diet, was another member of the pea family. It looks like what we call *vetch*, which is also in that family. We watched bears dig up the roots and eat them along the banks of the Savage River.

At lower elevations, the plants were bigger and grew in larger bunches than they did at Savage River. For those of you who read *Into the Wild*, Chris McCandless ate Eskimo potato seeds, and it is thought they might have contributed to his death. The seeds are edible, but the ones he had developed some kind of fungus or mold that prohibited digestion of food. I have given these plants a very good sniff, and for the life of me I can't tell what the bears see in them, but then, I am not much for veggies. I will eat a carrot if it is cooked in beef juice, or pretty much anything covered in gravy. Instead of wild plants, I would prefer some roasted Ptarmigan or maybe some sautéed Snowshoe hare.

"A flower's structure leads a bee toward having pollen adhere to its body ... we don't know of any such reason why beautiful places attract humans."

Although we knew that flowers needed rain, it had been raining for too many days in a row. It was not only raining, it was also cold. When we looked out the trailer window in the morning, we saw that at higher elevations, the rain was white and accumulating on the mountain tops. Val was considering writing a book called *Things to do in Denali Park in the Rain*. It would include chapters like: Test Your Rain Gear, Hike Along the Riverbed Because You're Wet Anyway, Fire-Starting Contests Can Be Fun, Cooking Supper in the Rain, Puddle Jumping—An Olympic Event, and How Close to the Road Can You Stand Without Getting Splashed by a Passing Tour Bus?

Lupine

Fireweed

Eskimo Potato

One day, as Val was taking me for a walk, she spied a three-toed woodpecker. Actually, I stopped for a sniff and so Val stopped and she heard this tap, tap, tap. When she investigated the noise, she found this sweet, little woodpecker. She didn't know it was a three--toed woodpecker until she got back to camp. If she had known it was a three-toed woodpecker she would have gotten a better picture of his toes.

Gray jays could be seen and heard every day. They were always ready to swoop in if there was any food to be seen. Liz Nestor made a pound cake and covered it with a yummy blueberry sauce made from berries picked near Savage Campground. She brought it over to share; there was just enough for everyone to have a slice. Val was standing and holding her plate of cake and looking for a seat when a gray jay swooped down and took her cake. What a rascal! We heard that they store food in trees to help them through the winter. We wondered where Val's slice of cake ended up.

Between the raucous calls of the magpies and ravens, there was no sleeping in, but Val loved the magpies especially. She talked about how smart they were and their ability to recognize themselves in a mirror. They mated for life but were known to display adulterous behavior during breeding time. The male often stood guard over his mate to keep other males away.

Val also told me there was even such a thing as a magpie funeral. When a magpie discovered a dead magpie, it would call loudly to attract other magpies. They would gather and call out loudly for a while and then disperse.

I believed these stories because the magpies in Savage Campground were continually making noise. I tried to pick up as much as I could of their language. They were pretty smart, but of course not as smart as yours truly. Just so you know, some of their conversations were pretty racy.

Ravens held a significant presence in Savage Campground and, for that matter, all of Alaska and the northwest coast of the North American continent. They were of the same family as the magpies and jays, but bigger. A raven was bigger than a crow, more the size of a hawk. They were pure black from their beaks to their toes.

I think they are competitive as well, because early in the morning I would hear them shouting back and forth with the magpies and the jays. The ravens would shout and tease the other birds, and then they would *nah nah nah* back at other ravens. It was all very tiresome.

The indigenous people have various myths about the raven being a creator of the earth and as a trickster god. Hunters believed that the raven would lead them to game, and that the ravens did so in order to receive a share after the animal was harvested. Like their human friends, they are omnivorous and can be found at the northernmost community of Barrow, Alaska, feeding at the dump. Humans say ravens are very smart birds. That may be true, but when they tried their tormenting routine with me, I just ignored them and hoped they would get bored and fly away.

Savage Camp had a center road with two loops coming off to the east and west. Our campsite was in the center of the west loop and went from the center road all the way over to the back of the west loop road. As we exited the trailer for an after-supper walk, the first decision was to go east or to go west.

East it was! My nose hit the ground before we even got past the end of the trailer. Once we passed the truck, there was another decision: right or left on the center road? Val gave me a little "gee" tug on the leash and off we went toward the entrance to Savage River Campground and the park road. Between our site and the park road, there were no other campsites. I was so happy to be out on a walk, I was wagging my tail and just sniffing along. *Let's see ... snowshoe hare, snowshoe hare, the neighbor's dogs, red squirrel, human, human ... this was so much fun.*

I was just doing my thing when I suddenly got a whiff of something different. It was strong—and it was wild. I began to follow the smell, of course, when Val pulled me back. I gave her my pleading look to say, *Val, you don't understand. This is something really fresh and amazing.* Although she eased up a little on the leash, she said, "No, Remington. You can't go off of the road." *Are you kidding me? I'm trying to tell you that some kind of wild thing has very recently been in this spot, right here. The smell is so wild and so different that my hackles are up!*

When Val noticed the hair on my back was standing straight up, she began to look toward where I was sniffing. "Yikes!" she said. "It's a lynx!"

I didn't see it because it blended into the background, but I could sure smell it. Val scooped me up and ran back to the trailer. "Dave, Remington found a lynx! I'm going back to see if I can get a picture. Wanna come?"

To a human, a picture is worth a thousand sniffs. When Val got back to the spot, sure enough the lynx had moved on, but she found him again, on the opposite side of the road. She was so excited with her picture, but of course, she never would have seen it in the first place if it had not been for her own Lynx Locator, aka Remington Beagle.

One evening, when Dave was doing a walk-about, he stopped across from campsite 1 to look at a dead tree the park service had marked to cut down. He heard a noise that sounded like a "huff" and turned to see what it was. There were two grizzlies in the road about twenty feet from him. They had stopped and were looking right at him, so he raised his clipboard in the air and shouted, "Get out! Get out - bears!" Just at that moment, a park service employee entered the park in his Jeep, which encouraged the bears to move on. As the bears moved past Dave into the campground, Dave yelled at a family grilling outside, and they grabbed their two young children and got inside their RV. He asked the guy in the Jeep to go to the end of the campground where there were Boy Scouts cooking supper and warn them. Two girls came to our host site and warned Val that they saw two bears by the toilet building. Val grabbed me, shoved me inside the trailer, and grabbed her camera. The bears snooped around the park a little and then headed on their way. All I got was the afterglow sniff of where they had been.

Dave loved to walk down to the river from the campsite and snoop around. Every chance he got, he was walking along the riverbank or crossing the river to see what he could find. When he turned around to come back to the campsite, this is the view he saw.

One morning, Dave and Val discovered bear pawprints going up the outside of the bathroom wall. It looked like a bear had walked up the wall with his front paws and looked in the window. The window was quite high, so it must have been a good-sized bear. Apparently, we had a peeping Tom bear in the park. What I meant to say was that we had a bear that was a peeping Tom, not a bare peeping Tom … never mind.

The bluff at the end of the campground near the river turned out to be Val's favorite spot. When we first arrived at Savage Campground, Val was a little nervous to be out at the end of the bluff by herself because it was far enough away from most campsites that no one would hear her if she was in need of help, but she was forced to go out there alone sometimes due to her responsibilities as a campground host. When she was out there, her senses were on high alert. She was continually watching and listening for signs of wildlife, especially the kind that might be a threat to safety. With some anxiety, she left the path and ventured out onto the bluff where she could see mountains on every side. The vista just opened up out there, and she felt very small and insignificant. Each time she was out on the bluff alone, she could hear a bird singing its heart out. She would pause and listen to this sweet distinctive voice, but she could never locate the bird. Then, one day, perched on the edge of a branch, was a sparrow with a black ring around its round white head singing away. Val had located the source of the symphony. The sparrow was singing a song of love to remind Val she was safe. *You are not alone, you are safe in God's hands.* The bluff became Val's cathedral; a perfect place for prayer. The White-crowned sparrow was her choir.

CHAPTER 17

FOUR WHEELING AND EXPLORING

"The first lesson is: life doesn't give you seat belts. And then: Always be yourself ... unless you can be Batman."
                                                                    The Lego Batman Movie

When Val and Dave's kids came to visit us in Alaska, it was fun times! My human sister Kym and her husband, Luke, visited our home in the wilderness. Luke was born in Alaska and felt at home here. Luke loved the outdoors, and especially Alaska.

Luke, Kym, and Val chose a fun excursion on all-terrain vehicles. North of the park was a place called Black Diamond, where you could golf or take an ATV ride. (Golf was a great attraction in Alaska because you could get a midnight tee time during the summer.) Before renting an ATV you had to watch a movie and pass a safety test. Val rode with Kym, and Luke drove his own. Val reported that the ride was fun, with stops at Dry Creek and at the top of a bluff overlooking Otto Lake and Healy, Alaska. By the time the group got back to Black Diamond, they looked like black diamonds. Boy! Were they ever dirty.

Back at camp, they had to clean up because that night was the Employee Appreciation Dinner. Dave and Val entered free as employees, and tickets were purchased for Kym and Luke. There was prime rib, shrimp, halibut, and much more. The dinner was scrumptious, but Dave and Val had to get back at camp so their co-hosts could also enjoy the dinner.

Leaving Dave, Luke, and me in charge of camp issues, Kym and Val went back into Riley Creek for a hike around the trestle. They chose a trail to the trestle instead of the steep sliding climb down from the railroad tracks. Val pointed out the old stone foundations, and Kym found the old pail Dave had seen. They met a young woman named Maggie sitting on the wooden footbridge near the trestle. She was waiting for her husband, Ted, to come down from the top of a huge rock sitting on the top of a hill behind us. He had been up on the rock for a half hour or more. Kym said, "Why don't you just holler up at him to come down?" Maggie said that she didn't think her voice would carry that far. Kym shouted, "Hey, Ted. Your time's up. Your wife wants you to come down." He waved, picked up his pack, and immediately headed down the rock. Maggie said, "Wow! Thanks a lot. He never would have heard me." Kym (the bullhorn Reynolds) said, "No problem." Maggie told Kym that they were recently married and only just arrived from Anchorage by train. They were on their honeymoon. Val said that explained why he jumped up so quickly and headed down the rock. If they had been married for any length of time, he would still be up there pretending he hadn't heard the summons.

Back at camp, I was happy when Val said, "Remington, time to go to work." We walked the campground and talked with many interesting people. We met the Altaris. Italians are so polite; they are so cultured.

The Altaris were not the only tourists with culture I met. I was having a grand time sniffing along the path, when a human walked by with a gorgeous, and I mean *gorgeous*, poodle.

Hello Dolly!
Bark, bark.
I love you too, sweetheart. If I could get off this leash, I would come over and give you a good sniffing.
Bark, bark.
Oh, baby. I'm pulling with all my might, but my human won't let me get near you.
Bark, bark.
Don't leave me, beautiful. Wait for me. Val, what are you thinking?! Don't you see that gorgeous babe getting away from me?
"Remington, quit pulling," said Val.
Are you out of your mind? I'm trying to catch up with that sweet little thing.
"Remington, we are going to sit right here until you calm down," Val said.
Calm down? Not in this millennium! Not with that beautiful girl dog up ahead. I can't even see her anymore. I will have to be satisfied with her scent. Maybe if I pull on the leash hard enough we can catch up with her.
Val was holding me back, and I was just as insistent to plunge ahead and find my girlfriend. Sniff, sniff … *there's her* smell. *Wow!* Sniff, sniff … Humans, with their diminished sense of smell, do not have a clue what we experience when we go on a sniff. When we meet another animal, that's how we get to know them. Sniffing private parts seems rude to humans, but that's our equivalent of shaking hands. There are times when I enjoy sniffing the trail where another dog has been even better than an actual experience with another dog. It's a good thing, because that was all I would have today. *My little poodle was gone, but her scent … was she wearing Estée Lauder? Ooh-la-la!*

There was another thing about humans that I don't get. When I left a pile in the park, Val immediately scooped it into a plastic bag and threw it in a trashcan. Poop was evidently a bad thing for humans because whenever I found a lovely smelling pile left by another dog, Val would say, "Yucky, Rem," and pull me away. *Yucky? Not at all. Poop told me so much. This one was either a poodle or a pug. Just take a whiff of this one ... I'm calling it Labrador ... it's big and moist and smells of duck feathers. Heaven.*

I found the varied requests we got as campground hosts interesting. There were lots of requests for matches, some requests for can openers and cork screws. Lots of folks who come in rented RVs were clueless as to how they worked. One day, a tenter came by with a camp stove in his arms. He wanted to know if we could show him how it worked. I wondered why anyone would wait until they were out in the wilderness to ask that question.

Yippee! Yahoo! Strike up the band. Val has completed 100 miles walked in Denali Park and Preserve. She will receive a free t-shirt documenting the event for her efforts. Dave, of course, has earned two t-shirts, and is working on a third. Over achiever!

T-shirts are not the only perks employees received. Dave and Val got a coupon with their check stub one week for pizza and a pitcher of beer at Denali Bluffs. The coupon was for the Mountaineer Grill, which is a little lower on the mountain than the fancy-schmancy Alpenglow, but the offer was a good one nonetheless, and it gave Val an opportunity to see some of the resort perched high on the mountain. She had been anxious to see it up close since we arrived.

The day they went to the Mountaineer Grill was rainy like all the days had been lately, but the views were spectacular anyway. I knew they felt heavy guilt for leaving me behind in the trailer, dining on Kibble, while they were living it up with pizza and beer. Val tried to make me feel better when they returned by saying, "Remington, you are way better than pizza and beer. You are more like filet mignon and baked potato."

CHAPTER 18

DENALI HIGHWAY AND VALDEZ

"The water you touch in a river is the last of that which has passed, and the first of that which is coming; thus it is with time."   *Leonardo da Vinci*

Another day found us traveling south on the Parks Highway. We loaded up with fuel and snacks in Cantwell, Alaska, before beginning our adventure on the Denali Highway. We had heard a lot about this trip, like be sure your gas tanks are full, you have a good spare tire, and rental companies will not allow their vehicles to be driven on this seasonal road.

It was 134 miles from Cantwell to Paxson on the Richardson Highway. We planned to take Richardson south to Valdez. The first three miles from Cantwell were paved and uneventful. Dave pulled over to try his luck at fishing at a small roadside pond. Val and I did a little walk/sniff about while he was fishing.

I found a treasure, and while Val was mountain gazing I was getting my shiny black proboscis into some awesome smelling … moose! Moose it was. Val turned to look at me and said, "Eeew! Remington! Yucky!"

I think not! It's a hoof and part of a leg bone. There was, of course, a moose smell, but as strong as the moose scent was the smell of wolves. Wolves had been eating at this, and I think I get a whiff of eagle too. I could have spent the day right here, but once again Val did not get it, and I was pulled away.

Next thing you know, we saw the real McCoy, and alive too! Val got out to take a picture. Inside the truck, hanging my head out of the window, I whined to get the attention of this moose, but to no avail. I was invisible to him. He could not be bothered with a beagle. Sometimes these guys are just too full of themselves. I told him that my relatives, the wolves, had made short order of his relative just down the road, but he could not be threatened, and in a huff he ran into the bush.

Denali Highway was conceived in the 1930s as a way to connect visitors to (at that time) Mount McKinley National Park, but funding was not available until after World War II, and construction didn't begin until the 1950s. Prior to the highway being built, the only way to the park was by railroad. The Denali Highway opened in 1957, and then the Parks Highway opened in 1972. Those travelers who came by car beginning in 1957 had to have a strong desire for adventure. It was very difficult to get to Alaska by car back then, and from there on to the national park by car was even more difficult.

Currently there are signs that warn there might not be any help if you get stranded, and the road has a reputation for roughness, so why would anyone want to travel such a road? I can tell you that I hate a tickle-butt road as much and maybe more than most, but the trip was definitely worth it. We traveled along at the recommended thirty-five-miles per hour, scanning the road for hazards, but also viewing glaciers flowing down from the heights of the Alaska Range, the beautiful Susitna River, moose, caribou, and a fox. The mountains and the glaciers are ok, but personally I get really excited about seeing wildlife. I'm a city dog after all, and the only wild things I see at home are an occasional skunk, raccoon, or opossum. I get pretty wound up at the sight of a moose, caribou, or even a fox. At one point we stopped, and Dave and Val were trying to get me to look toward the front of the truck. I was trying to communicate that there were three caribou at the side of the road behind the truck, while Dave and Val were trying to get me to look another caribou in front of the truck. They finally got my message, and did they ever feel silly. *Those two really must work on their situational awareness!* Back on our journey, the road took us to the second highest highway pass in the state, but from Maclaren Summit to Paxson, it was all downhill.

Denali Highway

Alaska Range & Glacier

We had already traveled the road from Paxson to Glenallen, and it was just as enjoyable as the first time. Glenallen to Valdez was different and exciting. Our route through the Thompson Pass was the same route taken by all overland travelers to Valdez. There was only one land route in and only one land route out of Valdez, and it was the same road.

Most mountain passes are made up of curves and heights, but in the Thompson Pass, they are to the superlative. There were places where it seemed the road would take us straight into the mountainside.

I had a vision of the road ending with a wall of mountain in front of us where the road should go. Maybe we would say, "Abracadabra," and the mountain would then magically open for us to continue on to our destination. But just when we thought that the road was bound to end abruptly, there was another curve and new vistas. There were places where the road traveled the deepest part of the valley, and the sides of the mountain rose so steeply on either side that it felt like we were in a tunnel, but stretching your sight to the top of the crevice there was blue sky. The waterfalls were spectacular. I have traveled with Val and Dave along stretches of road where Val will entertain herself with a book. This was not one of those roads. This was a road where the eye moves from one serendipitous sight to another, and you can't wait for the next turn and view.

I was happy when we got to Valdez, and I could get out of the truck for a walk and a sniff. One side of Valdez was perched at the edge of a protected ocean bay, and the opposite side snuggled against the mountain. It was the terminus of the Trans Alaska Oil Pipeline that originated in Prudhoe Bay. Ships came through Prince William Sound to Valdez to load up with oil they delivered to ports around the world. Fishermen also made their living out of this port. And there were many choices for tourists who wanted to go fishing, and for tourists who only wanted a boat ride out into the sound, there was the *Lu Lu Belle*. The *Lu Lu Belle* was small enough to give guests a close view of the many wonders in the area around Valdez.

The first wildlife we saw from the *Lu Lu Belle* were adorable sea otters floating on their backs. Further out into Prince William Sound, we saw fishermen, seals, and stellar sea lions. We got very close to the Columbia Glacier, a large tidewater glacier, watched the glacier calve. *I was relieved that my motion sickness was conquered, and I loved a good boat ride.* We saw the spot where the Exon Valdez went aground. The oil spill caused by that grounding resulted in massive damage to the sound. It killed sea birds, seals, killer whales, sea otters, and bald eagles. Thank goodness that now, twenty plus years later, it looks beautiful, and the wildlife is back. However, the destruction from the 1964 earthquake can still be seen.

The epicenter of the 1964 earthquake that hit Alaska was seventy-eight miles east of Anchorage. It was huge, with a magnitude of 9.2. There was tremendous damage in Anchorage, but the tsunami that came as a result of that earthquake destroyed Valdez. It caused an underground landslide, and part of the city's shoreline sank into the sea and wiped out the docks. It took three years to completely move the town to its current site on more stable ground.

Valdez is a small town. It was enjoyable to walk around the marina and it was fun to peruse the shops and museum. The people were nice and it was interesting to see the rabbits wandering all over town.

Rabbits could be seen as prevalent as squirrels back home. If I only could have been released from the tether between me and Dave; I could have done some serious rabbit hunting. Leash laws are such a nuisance. It's a shame that a few unmannered dogs have ruined it for all of us gentlemen beagles. My awareness of the distance I was allowed to travel

Tolsona Creek

resulted in my ignoring the rabbits for the most part. If you can't chase them it just takes all of the fun out of it. For fun we visited the museum, and it had a lot of information on the earthquake and tsunami. On your way there, you can stop and get an ice-cream cone. I like vanilla, with sprinkles.

The distance between Valdez to Glenallen was the same as the trip from Glenallen to Valdez, only in reverse. From Glenallen to The Tolsona Campground on Tolsona Creek was new road for us and was worth the trip. Tolsona was our kind of campground. You had to drive off the highway on a two-track to reach it, but once there, it was heaven.

Tolsona Creek runs through the campground and most sites are right on the creek. Dave likes to have campfires, and there were firepits on each site. What I like about having a campfire is that it is a magnet to humans. There's something primordial about humans and a campfire. They tend to gather and connect around the light and the warmth. It's kind of like leaving your porchlight on for Halloween. It says "open for business." Next thing you know, someone is walking up to your campsite and saying hi. We have met a lot of cool people around a campfire; from every occupation you can think of, from truck drivers to teachers and technicians and world travelers.

Beagles are natural pack animals, and it doesn't have to be with other dogs. We willingly "pack" with humans just as easily. On one of our excursions to Tolsona, Lisa, Randy, and Grandma Marge were with us. It was raining, but we had firewood to use up because it was nearing time for us to go home. Dave was not going to let a little thing like rain stop him from having his campfire. He did get a nice fire going in the firepit and sat there by himself in the rain. Grandma felt sorry for him, and went out to sit by the fire, but took an umbrella with her. Next thing you know, Lisa and Randy appeared from the campsite next door. That shamed Val and me to join this menagerie that didn't know enough to come in out of the rain. As we were chatting and having adult cocktails, Grandma got to laughing and tipped her umbrella to just the exact angle where some collected rainwater went right down her back. The humans thought this was hilarious. Unlike humans, dogs respect their elders. Val said she loves me more than a toasted marshmallow.

CHAPTER 19

SKAGWAY

"The mountains are calling, and I must go."   *John Muir*

Skagway is a community often seen by tourists coming off of cruise ships that dock there for the day. Dave and Val have cruised to Alaska; just the two of them the first time, and with family the second. Both times they enjoyed the White Pass Railroad ride. The White Pass Railroad ride is educational as well as scenic and entertaining. Val said that they took the ride all the way into Canada and back again. They didn't need passports because they did not get off the train.

The train took them along the route that the gold stampeders took to get to the gold fields. The would-be miners took ships to Seward and then went either up through White Pass or they went to Dyea (pronounced *die-yee*), and up the Chilkoot Trail. During the Gold Rush, there were many good people who risked everything for riches in gold. There were also some not-so-good people who deceived, stole, and took advantage of others in any way they could. One of the not-so-nice people that lived in Skagway was Soapy Smith. He was reportedly called Soapy because he ran a scam with bars of soap and dollar bills.

On the outskirts of town was the cemetery, and a grave located just outside the boundary of the cemetery marked Jefferson Smith was Soapy's. After hearing about what a nasty character he was, you know what I wanted to do on his grave, but Val pulled me away. She said that no matter what reputation a person had in this life, you never, never desecrate a grave. I made do with a ditch.

A breathtakingly beautiful way to get to Skagway is by road. Just turn at Jake's Corners off of the Alaska Highway and follow the sights to Skagway. The drive from Carcross to Skagway has to be the most beautiful stretch of highway in the world. We saw the lake the stampeder's navigated on their way to the gold fields. We saw a snowshoe hare and a grizzly bear. Traveling through a mountain pass it's up, up, up, and then down, down, down to sea level. Going down, we got a glimpse of the harbor, with cruise ships lined up right at the edge of town. Suffice it to say, it was a pretty sight.

Fuel is a subject at the forefront when traveling this part of the world. Skagway had only one gas station—and only one pump. Needless to say, there was not much competition nearby, so the fuel was not cheap. We were happy to get it nonetheless.

We also visited Dyea and the Chilkoot Trail. Prior to the gold rush of the 1890s, Dyea was a small Tlingit village. Big ships from the south could sail into Skagway because it was a deep-water port. In order to get closer to the Chilkoot Trail, the prospectors took smaller boats to Dyea, and at Dyea they could get the supplies they needed to head up the trail.

There is a current road from Skagway to Dyea, and it was scenic. In many places, the road was built right on the edge of the water. It was a one-lane road, so we had to keep our eyes peeled for oncoming traffic and places to pull over far enough to let another car pass. We continued on past the town and the trail and drove for miles along a two-track without seeing any other signs of civilization. I loved it—my kind of place. The smells were especially great when we stopped to walk around. Wild animal smells I could not even identify and some great piles of grizzly scat. My nose was working so hard and fast it's a wonder I didn't sprain it. We could hear fast-moving water, but we couldn't see it from the road. We hiked in a bit and found a waterfall. After we poked around in the wilderness, we got back in the truck and returned to the historic town of Dyea.

The town was built on the edge of the flats. Some rotting posts out at the end of the flats were evidence of an old dock. We walked out on the flats, but it was very windy, so we decided to check out the old town site. Pretty much all that was left is a false store front in one area, and piles of rotting lumber in another place identified as a former warehouse.

On the way out of the town, we took a side trip to the Slide Cemetery. On April 3, 1898, an avalanche on the Chilkoot Trail killed seventy people. More than half of them were buried in Slide Cemetery. Most of the graves in the cemetery were dated April 3, 1898, but one said that the man was shot in the mountains and died May 1, 1898. While we were walking around in the cemetery, we heard a tour guide

tell his group that only about one tenth of one percent of the tourists drive out to see the flats at Dyea. I guess they're too busy in the jewelry stores in town. As for me, I prefer the flats. A beagle can run and sniff all kinds of stuff when the tide is out. It was one of the places where I was off leash and could run and sniff to my hearts' content. Just call me an old mud-flat sniffer.

Down the road, we saw a sign for the Chilkoot Trail. We had to check it out. For about the length of a city block, the trail was in the open and next to the river. It was peaceful. The trail itself was hard and rocky with few smells, but it soon became more interesting. Boreal forest surrounded us, turning daylight into a dusky, dank scene. The trail got narrow and small rocks turned to large boulders we had to navigate. We stopped a moment to get our bearings. Yes, this was the trail. It got ever steeper and more difficult. *People brought mules up this thing?* It felt like we were the only civilized life for miles.

We started to feel antsy, not knowing what kind of wildlife we might encounter, so we turned to go back to the truck. We would never make good stampeders. Actually, I would have continued up the trail, but Val had the leash, so I had to follow her. Val called me Remington the Intrepid. I'm not sure what that meant, but I think it was good.

CHAPTER 20

HOPE AND WHITTIER

"Life is not a spectator sport. If you're going to spend your whole life in the grandstand just watching what goes on, in my opinion, you're wasting your life."　　　*Jackie Robinson*

Hope, Alaska, is a small, artsy, friendly, and historical community. It was one of the early gold-rush towns. People say they liked the campground because it was relaxing. Actually, it was the rules that were relaxed. Kids and dogs ran wild, and everybody looked after them. The campground typically fills up late in the day. At nine o'clock at night you can still see people setting up tents out on the flats.

We arrived early and found a pull-through site. There was room for the trailer but only a couple feet at the most on either side, and we could not get the big slides all the way out. We found the electric hook-up on a post between our site and the one next to us. It was a 110 outlet, like what you would find in a house. We later learned that if our neighbor was making toast we would blow a fuse if we turned on a light. This was how the campground encouraged goodwill among campers. If you didn't cooperate with your neighbor, you could forget about having any electricity. On the plus side, if you needed to borrow a cup of sugar, you could just reach out a window and tap on the neighbor's trailer. No need to even go outside!

There were lots of people camping in tents and some even slept in their cars. There were fishermen, hikers, prospectors, music lovers, and people who just like to camp. People started conversations as if they already knew you.

"Hey, that's a nice lookin' beagle. Don't ya think he's a little too heavy?"

"Did ya hear if there's gunna be any music tonight at the bar?"

If aliens dropped in from outer space, these friendly folks would not miss a beat. "Don't worry about your spaceship—just leave it right there. Is that your dog? Oh, I'm sorry. You say it's your mother-in-law? I understand, no really I do. You should see mine."

The Hope Campground is located on the Turnagain Arm, where the Resurrection River empties into the Arm. This river is noted for the salmon run; so, Dave and I walked over to the river. Dave had only four more days left on his fishing license. We saw people fishing, but no fish. People said it could be another week yet.

The tides here are significant. As the tide comes in, the rising water actually reverses the flow of the river. It was something to see.

The next day we headed inland along the river to find a spot where it was legal to do recreational mining. There were actual gold miners there. One guy even had a portable dredge. He told us that he paid $2,500 for it, and expected to make that much before the end of the season.

Dave and Val's investment consisted of a pail, a shovel, and a gold pan. Dave worked hard for hours, shoveling up river dirt and rocks and using the pan to see if he could find gold. I can confidently report that they lost money on their investment. I, however, had a great time running along the river's edge. The smells were fantastic.

We left the river and drove back to see more of Hope. Hope was named after one of the early prospectors, Percy Hope. We met an old guy at the museum who looked like he might have known Percy personally. He knew everything about the town. We bought a "poke" from him (a small bag of dirt with some gold in it) and had much better luck panning that. You could actually see the gold. But, once again, we were in the hole in terms of investment, although not in terms of fun.

Between the campground and the Turnagain Arm of Cook Inlet was a flat grassy area that used to be the location of the town. The 1964 earthquake caused the ground to drop so the residents moved the town to higher ground to avoid flooding during high tides.

Val and I enjoyed walking along the flats. It was one of our favorite activities. One evening as we were walking, some nice young people came near us with some Labrador Retrievers. I was on a leash, and these dogs were loose. Crazy loose. They were jumping and running all over. One of the young people said to Val, "Why don't you let your dog run?" I'm thinking, *Yes! Yes!* But Val said, "I don't think so." The wonderful young man said, "Oh, let him go. He will have a great time." Serendipitously, Val said, "Well, ok."

Wow! Off I went after the two Labradors. The grass was taller than me so occasionally I would jump up and look back just to be sure Val was still there. Those two boys were twice my size, but I kept up with them. We would run full tilt through the tide pools and the grass. I couldn't remember when I had so much fun. Labradors are known in the dog world as being free thinking and fun.

It was over all too soon, and when we got back to the trailer, Dave took one look and said, "He is not coming in the trailer until he has a bath." *A bath? Is there a dog groomer in Hope?* Unfortunately not. I ended up in the Resurrection River. That was some kind of dog cruelty, I can tell you—apparently the price I had to pay to play.

On the Fourth of July, we decided to drive from Hope to Whittier for their Fourth of July parade. We made a stop at the visitor's center at Portage Lake, and Val got some pictures of the icebergs in the lake. From there, we went through a short tunnel before coming to the Whittier Tunnel. The Whittier Tunnel is a tunnel for trains that cars use when the trains are not present.

After paying a toll, we got in lane one and waited for the next release time. When lane one for cars and small trucks was full, cars began to line up in lane two. People got out of their cars even though the directions told us to stay in our cars. One guy went off into the woods and came back with a rock so big he could hardly carry it. He deposited it in his car and went back for another. Then another guy marched past all the signs that said "Absolutely NO Pedestrian Traffic," and "Authorized Personnel Only." This was making Dave and Val crazy because they are retired government people, and rules are rules.

Finally, the light for lane one turned green and we were off like a shot. It's a little bizarre driving a car on railroad tracks, even though the road was built up to the edge of the tracks and the traveling was pretty smooth. We drove for 2.6 miles on the tracks before we came to the other side of the mountain. We were finally in Whittier.

Whittier was established by the U.S. Army during World War II as a secret port. Today it is a historic landmark. Whittier's port does not freeze over in the winter so it was useful for all kinds of shipping. Following the war, the Army built two large buildings that still remain in Whittier. One of the buildings still houses 80 percent of the residents of Whittier. We were not sure where the other 20 percent lived because we did not see even one house in town. Maybe they lived on boats. Whittier was pretty much boats and trains, and sometimes the two merged as evidenced by the U.S. Coast Guard Auxiliary Station being housed in an old train car.

We made it just in time for the parade. Every emergency vehicle in town was pressed into service, along with a float from the Donut Depot, and a string of Corvettes. They did not have one beagle in their parade. *Really?! All they had to do was ask.* What the parade lacked in pizzazz, it made up for in enthusiasm. It snaked through every street in town (about four), and people on the sidelines shouted support and waved flags. How much fun was that!

Too soon, our tour of Whittier completed, we were back in line to return to Portage and beyond through the train tunnel. As luck would have it, a train was also in the lineup. Since it was, after all, a train tunnel, the train got to go first. The sign told us that we would get a release time as soon as the train cleared the tunnel. It was raining pretty hard, so people stayed in their cars this time. Before we knew it, we were through the tunnel and on our way to points unknown.

On our return to Hope Campground, Val rubbed my ears and called me handsome. She said I was more handsome than Elvis Presley—whoever that is.

CHAPTER 21

KENAI

"The love for all living creatures is the most notable attribute of man."
                                                        Charles Darwin

Kenai, Alaska, was a very special place among so many special places. It is where the Athabasca Indians, called *Dena'ina*, lived more than two thousand years ago. The great Kenai River flows into the Cook Inlet there, and marine life abounds.

When the Russians arrived there, the Dena'ina moved inland for their own protection. Over the years, the Russian and American cultures have blended. Some Dena'ina have recognized the sadness of this loss and are working to renew their ancient heritage. As a result, the area is a mix of Athabasca (Dena'ina), Russian, and American cultures; making it unique.

There is a bluff that overlooks the end of the Kenai River where it meets Cook Inlet. On some days, you can see a constant movement of boats as they travel on high tide out to sea to fish, and back again to sell their catch at the processing plants along the river. This does not happen every day because the government regulates when they can fish, and some days are closed to fishing. When the salmon return to the river to spawn, there is a tent city along the beach were individual fishermen and their families camp and fish. There are times when the salmon can only be caught with a line and a reel, and other times when you are allowed to catch them with a net.

The bluff was also a prime spot for watching beluga whales. The best time to see one of these small white whales was two hours before and two hours after high tide. Dave had a tide schedule. He read that the tides at this time of year are about nineteen feet. We spent a lot of time on a bench on the bluff with binoculars and zoom lens on a camera looking for belugas. I was not excited about seeing a beluga from way up on a hill. The sniff factor would be nil. I did love lying in the grass and getting mysterious smells brought to me on the breeze. Did you know that eagles break wind in flight?

Val and I took a walk to the strand below the cliff. We strolled along the edge of the river for maybe half a mile and enjoyed this perspective of the river and the bluff. You must use all of your senses while walking a beach to notice the grit of the sand, the heavenly views of the water and the birds, and maybe a sea otter or a whale. The sounds of boats, people laughing, and sea gulls provided us with a song. The smells were among my favorites because they were such a fabulous mix of salt, water, fish, sea mammals, boats, grass, little critters who lived in the sand and silt, and … I really tried to sniff out a beluga for Val, but I kept getting saltwater up my nose.

At the entrance to the path that took us to the beach, was a Russian Orthodox Church. Val entered the Holy Assumption Church because she was curious and thought she might see some icons. Inside she was met by a Russian Orthodox priest, Fr. Thomas Andrew, who showed her everything but the area reserved only for priests. Russian fur traders were the first to introduce Christianity to the native Alaskans. There was a shortage of Russian priests, and the first missionaries came in 1794. The first church in Kenai was built in 1849. The current church, built between 1894 and 1896, was an example of Russian culture in south central Alaska. The church featured a bell tower with a distinctive crown-shaped cupola with the three-bar Orthodox Cross. Holy Assumption Church is the oldest standing Orthodox Church in Alaska. Its icons and religious artifacts were treasured for their connection to the Orthodox faith. The only Russian that I know is a Russian wolf hound. Although he has an accent and dialect, I don't have trouble communicating with him in basic dog. If he is any indication of the size of Russian humans - they are giants. He's a fun friend, and I fit nicely under him for protection from neighborhood bullies.

The Russian influence, even after all these years, is still visible in Alaska. I'm not sure if they have Beagles in Russia, but what I can say is that although dogs are normally not allowed in churches, we make pretty good Christians. I know I am one of God's creatures and very much loved by Him. In fact I am representative of one of his better creations. Just ask Val.

CHAPTER 22

SEWARD

Look deep into nature, and then you will understand
everything better.   Albert Einstein

The highway going south from Anchorage is called the Seward
Highway and skirts the Turnagain Arm. This was a dangerous but
beautiful drive, no matter how many times you have done it. It was
even pretty in the rain. There are pullouts along the road so that
travelers can stop to view beluga whales, as well as the spectacular
mountain and water combination that makes this trip so enjoyable.
The mountains rise steeply from the water on both sides, providing
breathtakingly beautiful waterfalls. At the water's edge, the mountains
are thickly forested with spruce, alders, and birch; and the shades of
green go from light-yellow-green to a rich green that is nearly black.
As the tree line thins and the ground cover goes from bush to moss,
browns, grays and russets are added to the palette. A few of the
mountains were green at the top, but most were tall enough to be
barren rock at the summit.

Along this route is the Alaska Wildlife Conservation Center. We
drove through it and looked at the animals from inside the truck. I
enjoyed it because I could stick my head out the window and see all
of the animals, like fox, wolves, bear, and bison; as well as get a pretty
good sniff. During the 1964 earthquake, this area dropped some
fifteen feet and saltwater seeped into the ground, killing the trees. It

was green now, but many dead trees were still visible. I was fascinated by the wolves. From a distance they looked playful, but I knew wolves were serious animals; so, I was happy to be in the truck. Some humans think they can pet anything. Beagles know better.

After a brief stop in Girdwood, where the Alyeska Ski Resort is located, we arrived at our destination: the Crow Creek Mine. For a small fee, prospectors are given access to the creek where mining is allowed. We hiked along a path that led to the creek. As I was built close to the ground, I was very aware that the plant life in the southern parts of Alaska is much more profuse than in the center and northern parts of the state – it is rainforest and jungle like. A bonus is that there are no snakes in Alaska and only one frog – and I have no worries about the possibility of coming across a frog. So our walk to the creek was worry free – we only had to think about grizzly bears, or maybe getting trampled by a moose. After finding the ideal spot, we dug the dirt, panned the dirt, and searched for gold in the pan. No luck. It was all about the experience. *Sure it was...*

There were many buildings on site, left from an old mining village. Some had tableaus showing furniture and utensils from long ago. There was a little spring at the side of the path with cans of soda floating in the ice-cold water. It was a self-serve beverage choice that had a small pail hanging nearby where you could pay for what you took. Perfect.

Back on the highway, and closer to Seward we found a heavenly place called Stoney Creek RV Park. It was nestled in the woods next to Stoney Creek. The glacier-fed creek and surrounding mountains made this a beautiful scenic spot. The pull-through sites were level with gravel, had fire pits, and small grassy areas. All of the sites were generously wide and some even backed up to the creek. The camp rules warned that this was bear country, and you must not leave any food or coolers outside and unattended. *Are beagles considered bear food?*

Not far from here was Exit Glacier. This glacier has been melting for centuries, and it was still pretty awesome. The Exit Glacier is part of the Harding Icefield. There was a great picture-taking opportunity from the road that encompassed the glacier from top to terminus. From the nature center there were options to hike and get close to the glacier. One of the trails goes midway up the glacier, where hikers can actually walk out onto the glacier. Another trail went along the river to the terminus. There was also an opportunity to take a ranger-led walk. Exit Glacier Park is open year-round. The area was closed to cars in the winter but open to snowmobiles and other winter fun, such as cross-country skiing and snowshoeing. Grandma Marge stood by a sign that showed where the terminus of the glacier was the year she was born.

On Old Exit Glacier Road, there are Alaska Creekside Cabins. Every cabin is located on the creek! The beauty of the surroundings was only exceeded by the hospitality of the owner. His name was Tim, and he was a really great guy. Every cabin was named and each one was different. I loved our little cabin, and don't tell Tim – Val threw a blanket on the bedspread and I slept on the bed all night. Tim built us a fire one night, and we had fun watching the salmon in the stream. The stream is small, and I was tempted to jump in and catch a salmon as they swam

by, but fishing was closed and you know how I feel about water.

The town of Seward is located on Resurrection Bay on the Kenai Peninsula of Alaska. There were many fun things to do and see in Seward, and one of them was the Kenai Fjords Tour.

There were various tours and times to choose from. If you choose one of the trips that takes you into Prince William Sound, be aware that the seas get rougher when you leave Resurrection Bay and enter the sound. Ask my human brother-in-law Luke. He got green around the gills just thinking about his trip out to the fjords. The water was calmer when you reached the fjord though, and when you watched a glacier calving, the experience made it all worthwhile.

Another excursion took us to Fox Island, in Resurrection Bay, for a lunch of prime rib and halibut. On the way to Fox Island, there were stops to see puffins and common murre, small birds that look like penguins but are not. For penguin sightings you need to travel significantly south from here. There were also cormorants, seals posing on rocks, and mountain goats.

Humpback whales are also commonly seen in the bay. What magnificent animals. When you search for humpbacks, you look for the spray they put up when they surface for air—it's called a spout. A spout can be seen many miles away. The spout is caused by the whale breathing the air out of its lungs. So, wherever there is a spout, there is a humpback whale. It is very exciting to see a whale breach, which is when they come completely out of the water. It is awesome! Nearly as exciting, is when they only come partway out and then on their way back down expose a view of their tail called a *fluke*. Every fluke is different; kind of like a whale fingerprint. Beagles have fingerprints too. It's their nose. (Couldn't resist a little trivia here.)

On one of our Kenai Fjord tours, my human sister Wendy could not resist a picture-taking opportunity riding an orca.

The Alaska Sea Life Center is worth a visit. It was the only place in Alaska that not only had an amazing aquarium; the staff also conducted marine research as well as provided response for wildlife in need. There were fish, birds, invertebrates, and marine animals. Opportunities were provided to learn about the salmon that are so prevalent in Alaska. Salmon are beautiful, especially compared to the wolf eel that is scary looking. I hope I never run into one of those in the wild. It's just another reason why I have a no-swim policy. The bird sanctuary at the center was also amazing. We had a close encounter with puffins and saw common eider ducks and harlequins. Downstairs were viewing windows into the aquarium where we could watch the sea lions and seals.

There is a mountain in Seward that used to be called Lowell Mountain, but is now called Mt. Marathon. The name was changed due to a race held on the mountain every Fourth of July. Locals will tell you the race was started when some good old boys in the bar bet that no one could run up the mountain and back down in an hour. The first runner lost the bet with a time of sixty-two minutes.

The race attracts more than 800 people each year, and winners usually finish in about forty-three minutes. The race distance is a little over three miles, with an elevation gain of 3,022 feet. The good news was that there was also a hiker's trail that is much easier, with some switchbacks. If you are walking and not racing, you can take time to enjoy the fabulous views of Seward, Resurrection Bay, the rocky islands, and the Kenai Mountains. I personally recommend the walk – it takes longer, but it is safer.

One of the best ways to travel the 470 miles from Seward to Anchorage was by train. The stretch between Seward and Anchorage was very scenic. Mountains and valleys, tunnels and sunsets, the Grandview Pass and the Turnagain Arm were wonderful sights seen from the dome car. There was even a café where you can purchase sandwiches and snack items; on some trains there was also a dining car for a more formal meal. The seating was comfy and the train was a great way to relax and enjoy the view while someone else did the driving.

CHAPTER 23

WILLOW AND WASILLA

"The whole concept of 'wild' was decidedly European, one not shared by the original inhabitants of this continent. What we called 'wilderness' was to the Indian a homeland, 'abiding loveliness' in Salish or Piegan. The land was not something to be feared or conquered, and 'wildlife' were neither wild or alien; they were relatives."   Doug Peacock

If you travel the Parks Highway from Denali National Park and Preserve south to Anchorage, you will pass through Willow, Alaska. (Once home to Luke Reynolds, my human brother-in-law.) Willow is where the Iditarod currently starts, and it is home to many mushers. It also was once thought of as a better place for the state capital than Juneau because it is more centrally located and more accessible to residents.

Like many places in Alaska, Willow was known for gold. Gold was found in Willow Creek in the late 1800s and, at one time, it was Alaska's largest gold-mining district. Personally, I like Willow for a break in traveling. Although I no longer get motion sickness, I do like a breath of fresh air and a little walk every now and then. It is true that I have superlative olfactory capabilities. However, as much as I have tried, and as much as Dave wishes I could, I have never been able to sniff out gold.

The next community heading south was Wasilla. Sarah Palin was once mayor of Wasilla, before she was elected governor of Alaska, and later chosen as Senator John McCain's running mate in the 2008 U.S. Presidential election. Wasilla was bigger than Willow and was also considered as a spot for the state capital, but it was voted down.

When the George Parks Highway found its way through Wasilla, around 1970, it put Wasilla directly on the roadway link from Anchorage to Fairbanks. There are many shopping opportunities in Wasilla, as well as places to camp; so, it is a great stop before heading north. There were some big-box stores in Wasilla, so we take the opportunity to shop where the selection was better and the prices were lower than farther north.

There's a campground in Wasilla called Ice Worm. The first time we saw it we thought the name was a joke. Later we found that there really is such a thing as an ice worm. There is Ice Worm Gulch in Denali Park. However, after finding pictures of ice worms online we have never been lucky enough to find one so I have no idea what they smell like. Val said that I am the garlic butter on her escargot.

CHAPTER 24

PALMER AND HATCHER PASS

"... and this is why the caribou and the wolf are one; for the caribou feeds the wolf, but it is the wolf that keeps the caribou strong."   *Farley Mowat*

Palmer, Alaska, is home to the Alaska State Fair. It is located just north of Anchorage in the Matanuska Valley where, due to nearly twenty-four hours of daylight in the summer, they grow huge cabbages and other vegetables. It was also the home of our friends Mike and Amy and their two beautiful girls who live on a small farm with their goats and wonderful dogs.

A drive up Hatcher Pass Road from Palmer is very scenic, with fun places to stop as the road winds upward to the abandoned Independence Gold Mine, which is now the Independence Mine State Historical Park. This is where we saw a hoary marmot next to the road. The window was down, and I did try to connect with this animal, but even though he tipped his head and I believe tried to understand me, the language barrier was just too wide. I sensed he meant me no harm, and the feeling was mutual.

The Independence Mine was a significant operation prior to World War II, when there was a halt in mining. Although the mining activity continued after World War II, production declined and the mine was closed in 1951. We enjoyed walking around the mine site and checking out some of the abandoned buildings. There were hiking trails that offered views of the area and the valley from higher up the mountain.

On our way down the mountain, we stopped at a musk ox farm. We walked on paths through fenced-in areas where the musk ox are close to the path. The farm also sold items made from musk ox yarn and the yarn itself. The yarn was expensive, but I'm sure it was not easy to harvest fibers from the aggressive musk ox. Val said she wished she could harvest my hair and make yarn. She said that with the amount of hair I left on everything, I should be bald. As far as I was concerned, she could brush me every day and do whatever she wished with the hair.

CHAPTER 25

ANCHORAGE

"The love for all living creatures is the most noble attribute of man."
                                                              Charles Darwin

The first time we visited Anchorage, we drove from Denali National Park and Preserve. We stayed at the Golden Nugget Campground in the city. It was the well-manicured parking-lot type of campground. We were amazed at the gorgeous and gynamic (my own word) hanging baskets of flowers. Sunlight nearly twenty-four hours a day in the summer does wonderful things for plants, just add water and boom—beauty to behold.

Another visit took us to an historic hotel in downtown Anchorage, just up the hill from the train station. It was the only hotel that survived the 1964 earthquake. Each room was different and lovely. On one visit, we were exhausted and went to bed about 8:30 p.m. because we wanted to be well-rested for our trip to Wasilla the next morning. All of a sudden Val woke up, looked at the clock, and announced that we had overslept and missed our train to Wasilla. We saw that it was daylight and the clock said 10:00. However, in Alaska during the summer, 10:00 p.m. is still a bright part of the day. We were fully awake before we realized that it was night and we had many more hours before our train left in the morning. Val felt very silly, but she had no trouble going back to sleep.

Another visit to Anchorage found our group camped by Ship Creek (without a paddle). This location made it handy to go down to the creek and watch the fish and the fishermen. As I have mentioned before, the tides in Alaska are monumental. We got a tide schedule and figured out when the high tide would be in and when it would be low tide. It was fun to take pictures showing the difference to prove to the people back in Michigan what we were experiencing.

A short distance out of the city, we found the Alaska Native Heritage Center where the major cultural native groups from Alaska are represented, such as Aleut, Alutiiq, Athabascan, Cupik, Eyak, Haida, Inupiaq, St. Lawrence Island Yupik, Tlingit, Tsimshian, and Yupik. The center of the state, near Denali, was home to the Athabascan people. They were the last native Alaskans to have contact with people from the outside because their habitat was so difficult to reach. Native young people perform native songs, dances, and games. Outside was a trail around Lake Tiulana where there were life-sized native dwellings to explore. The Hall of Cultures included a small museum of native history, and native artists that sold their goods. Val bought an interesting white-and-green necklace and earrings made from moose bones and jade. The local native woman who sold the necklace said that her husband had harvested the moose. The moose meat added to their larder, and they made use of everything – including the bones. I tried a sniff of the necklace, but I could not define any moose smell at all.

Another great place to find native art was the Anchorage Market and Festival which was held from May to September. It was an open-air market located at 3rd Avenue and E Street. There were great Alaskan artifacts for reasonable prices, as well as food and entertainment. One year, we saw the Human Juke Box there. Now that was something to experience.

Earthquake Park was interesting. The sharp drop-off at the north end of the park provided a clear view of how the land sank many feet in the 1964 earthquake. The rippling hills in the forest were also evidence of what happened during the 9.2 magnitude earthquake. The park is a popular place for runners and cyclists, as well as for tourists who just want to hike and view visual remnants of 1964. I loved walking and sniffing the paths. People run into bears here, but I didn't get any sniffs of bear while we were there. I sniffed out some interesting mushrooms, and wondered if they would be good sautéed in butter and served with some ptarmigan. I didn't get a chance to try them as we just looked, admired, and moved on. Val said that I am the truffles in her pork pie. Anybody know what she's talking about here?

CHAPTER 26

GOING HOME

"There is no mile as long as the final one that leads back home."
Katherine Marsh

Campground hosts were required to stay and work at the park through the time of the park road lottery if they wanted to be eligible for the season bonus. Travel on the park road was primarily limited to bus traffic during the summer season in order to protect and preserve wildlife, and also make it possible for visitors to the park to be able to view the park and the animals. Visitors were stopped at a checkpoint at the Savage River Bridge, and only those camping at one of the campgrounds past that point and other official business were allowed to pass. However, at the end of the season, the park offered a road lottery for the remaining number of trips permitted by law. The road lottery took place the second weekend after Labor Day. Those wishing to drive out into the park in their private vehicles applied via recreation. gov website after May 1, and winners were notified in June. Because it often snowed in Denali National Park and Preserve in September, the distance lottery winners were allowed to travel could be reduced due to bad road conditions.

Savage Campground was usually full during road lottery because it was a great starting point for a drive out into the park. As hosts, we were not only thinking about our full campground of guests, we were also thinking about a 4,000-mile trip home through the northern

Rocky Mountains—possibly in snow—pulling a fifth-wheel trailer. We were busy stowing things away for road travel and anticipating the end of our great adventure.

Leaving the park was a bittersweet event. We loved the park, and we had made connections with other hosts who we were also loath to leave. We decided to go as far as North Pole, Alaska, for the first leg of our trip, and then camp together as far as we could down the road.

It was cold and clear that night at North Pole, which was just south of Fairbanks. Val fell into bed early after days of packing and getting ready for traveling. Dave woke her up late in the evening for our first view of Aurora Borealis in Alaska. The northern lights were beautiful, and Val was happy to be awakened to see the wavy green lights in the night sky. Most of the time we were in Alaska the sky was too light to see northern lights. It started getting dark at night in August, but then it was so often cloudy we never saw the lights from Denali.

Our next stop was Border City, Alaska. We could get fuel, a hot shower, and even a sandwich there. After another night spent with our coworker hosts, the next morning it was a short trip to Customs and entry into Canada. My days of motion sickness behind me; I was nonetheless very happy to get out of the truck and have a run. Dave and I found a big field where I ran around and gave my nose a good workout, as well as my legs.

We always stop at Liard Hot Springs, both to and from, because it is such a favorite spot. After Liard, we are often searching for a place to camp at the end of the day because Dave likes to put miles behind us on the way home. When we discovered that Lion's Campground, where we usually stop at was full, we got directions to the next Lion's Campground down the road near Wonowan, British Columbia. It was perfect for us, with grassy sites and a field close by for beagles.

We enjoyed having our awning out and eating supper at the picnic table on our site. I loved walking the campground and checking out the other dog campers. I am especially fond of poodles, and there was this little white one that was so nice. I got to say hello to her—and it was some hello. Butt sniffing all around. It was an amazing evening and we all slept soundly in this little piece of paradise.

We had planned to get up early and get back on the road toward home, but the sleeping was so good we overslept. So we got up in a hurry and packed up. As we left the campground, we saw a man leave his trailer and run out to the road toward us. Unfortunately, he was just slightly late in his attempt to stop us as our awning (still fully out) hit a tree. Ouch. Boy, did we feel stupid. The nice man who tried to stop us was the campground host. He helped us get the awning back into place and secured for road travel. I guess in the future I will have to take inventory before we leave. A beagle's work is never done.

We were soon back in the U.S. and on our favorite highway, US-2. We were heading east and making time. Val said that I am like comfort food. Petting me is better than eating mac 'n cheese.

CHAPTER 27

HOME SWEET HOME

"God never ends anything on a negative; God always ends on a positive. Because what is negative about going home?"
                                        Shannon L. Alder

As we came full circle back to Michigan, we were compelled to stop at a special place. We have so many memories from time spent here that we would be remiss not to share some of them.

It ain't me, It ain't me, I ain't no fortunate son ..." is filtering through the woods into the campground from the Lumberjack Tavern. It was a fine evening; just cool enough for a campfire. The place was full tonight. Kim said she fills up almost every weekend. At nine o'clock it was just beginning to get dark, and people were starting to settle in for the night. The county park was perched on the edge of Lake Independence, and if you have forgotten your marshmallows and chocolate bars, the grocery store is within easy walking distance. The whole town was walkable from the campground, and the Lumberjack Tavern was just the other side of a strip of woods that ran between the road and the campground.

"The lake is beautiful tonight."

"It's been beautiful all day," Dave replied.

Kim had been managing the park for a long time. She and her husband, Jack, used to have a pet pig named Mrs. Perkins. Mrs. Perkins was not a teetotaler. She loved her beer. She would go from campsite to campsite and people would give her beer. When the campers all departed for the season, she was left without beer so she strolled over to the Lumberjack Tavern. The friendly drinkers let her inside and took turns buying her beer. By the end of the night, Mrs. Perkins would be passed out on the barroom floor. They couldn't leave her there because when she woke up alone she would tear the place apart. The only thing left to do was drag her outside, but she was a very big pig. Someone with a log chain and a pickup truck solved the problem, and soon Mrs. Perkins was back outside, none the worse for wear. Problem was that one of the good ole' boys couldn't help telling the story to people in Marquette, and very soon there was trouble in the happy kingdom of Big Bay. The "authorities" made it impossible for Mrs. Perkins to roam the park or the adjacent bar for beer. She had to be penned up and only given healthy things to eat. Needless to say, she went straight downhill from there and is no longer with us. Life for Mrs. Perkins was not worth living without roaming and carousing. She was buried at the spot where she was penned up. Even today, when I sniff around down by her pen, I get a faint hint of bacon. And beer.

One remnant from the 1950s was the old camp office, the same building you can see at the end of Otto Preminger's movie *Anatomy of a Murder*, with James Stewart and Lee Remick. It's historical, as is so much of this place. This is where the park manager lived and worked for many years. The new park office is located at the entrance of the park, and the park manager no longer lives in the park. Kim spent so many years in close proximity to campers that some nights, when the park was full, she woke up at daylight still in the park, sitting in her van in the parking lot. Dedication to duty like that is not easily found these days.

From the front yard of the cabin you can see the smokestack from the old Ford wood plant. Henry Ford had a plant in Big Bay to make the wood parts for his vehicles. You may, or may not, remember the station wagons with the shiny wooden doors and quarter-panels. Well, Big Bay is where the wood came from. He built the hotel in town, and Henry was a founding member of the Huron Mountain Club, which is still very exclusive and private. The club is located at the end of the Mountain Club Road. There is security at the gate, as well as roaming security ensuring no one trespasses on guests or wildlife on club property. We occasionally ride out the Mountain Club Road, and I think if Dave would let me out of the truck I could scoot in without notice and see what all the secrecy is about.

You get a view of people in a campground that you often do not get in a regular neighborhood. Things can be heard that are not meant to be heard by the world due to the close proximity of campers. Tones of voice can tell a whole story. When a man says, "I could use some help here," tone of voice is everything. Sometimes it's body language that's the illuminator. Like when some inexperienced person is backing a trailer into a spot, and has tried for the umpteenth time to get it where it needs to go and then hits a tree - when that guy gets out of the truck be assured that nothing needs to be said – his body language writes a book. I'm laying here on my leash right now watching some people across the road. The man is sitting in a chair. He is looking in the direction of the lake, drinking something out of a mug with one hand, and petting a dog with the other. Now that's human contentment if I ever saw it. We soon left contentment in Big Bay for the final leg of our trip to home.

The trip from Lake Independence to home is a familiar one, and as we near our final destination, time seems to drag. Like rented horses, all we want to do is get back to the barn. As we crossed the Mackinac Bridge heading south, we were hungry and tired, but we will not stop. As we opened the front door to our home in Traverse City, we had a sense of accomplishment. We feel contentment with a job well done and happy to be back near loved ones again.

Russell in Barrow, Alaska, was right. There's no place like home.